MAYANN FRANCIS

MAYANN FRANCIS

FRANCIS

An Honourable Life

Foreword by George Elliott Clarke

NIMBUS
PUBLISHING
—— NIMBUS.CA ——

Nimbus Publishing Limited
3660 Strawberry Hill Street, Halifax, NS, B3K 5A9
(902) 455-4286 nimbus.ca

Printed and bound in Canada

NB1398

Design: Jenn Embree
Editor: Marianne Ward
Proofreader: Elizabeth Eve
Photo research: Angela Mombourquette
For copyright/permissions information for materials quoted herein, see p. 201

Library and Archives Canada Cataloguing in Publication

Title: Mayann Francis : an honourable life / The Hon. Mayann Francis ; foreword by George Elliott Clarke.
Names: Francis, Mayann, author. | Clarke, George Elliott, writer of foreword.
Identifiers: Canadiana (print) 20189068558 | Canadiana (ebook) 20189068566 | ISBN 9781771087131 (hardcover) | ISBN 9781771087148 (HTML)
Subjects: LCSH: Francis, Mayann. | LCSH: Lieutenant governors—Nova Scotia—Biography. | LCSH: Stateswomen—Nova Scotia—Biography.
Classification: LCC FC2328.1.F73 A3 2019 | DDC 971.6/05092—dc23

Nimbus Publishing acknowledges the financial support for its publishing activities from the Government of Canada, the Canada Council for the Arts, and from the Province of Nova Scotia. We are pleased to work in partnership with the Province of Nova Scotia to develop and promote our creative industries for the benefit of all Nova Scotians.

I dedicate my story to my parents, who brought me into this world and prepared me for my journey. They gave me a solid foundation.

I also dedicate my memoir to my young grandniece Nevaeh O'Connell and her younger brother, my grandnephew Evander O'Connell, because I want my story to be an inspiration as people confront a variety of challenges in the present and in the future. I want my story to be an inspiration to encourage people to overcome whatever barrier they might face.

On January 22, 2019, my brother-in-law, Patriarch Vincent Waterman I, grandfather of Nevaeh and Evander, died. He left a legacy of caring, compassion, empathy, and love. He had an enduring love for his grandchildren. I would also like to dedicate this book to him.

Mayann Francis's grandniece Nevaeh O'Connell (left) and grandnephew Evander O'Connell. (COURTESY OF AUTHOR)

Mayann Francis's beloved brother-in-law, Archbishop Vincent M. Waterman. (SEAN O'CONNELL)

CONTENTS

TO HONOUR
HER HONOUR

Always direct (even curt), our American neighbours shorten "vice-president" to the informal "veep." If we work the same metamorphosis upon "vice-royal," perhaps we conjure up "vicar," a term relevant to Her Honour Dr. Mayann Francis, O.N.S., at least twice over. First, "vicar" is related to "vice," and signals, thus, her service as the vice-regal representative—or deputy—of Canada's constitutional monarch, i.e., Her Majesty the Queen. Secondly, "vicar" denotes a person who commands a church or chapel; for Ms. Francis, this word should remind her of her esteemed, Cuban-born father, George Anthony Francis, who, as Archpriest of St. Philip's African Orthodox Church in Sydney, Nova Scotia, infused his daughter with Christian courage, pride in her African heritage, and a seldom-errant moral compass. Certainly, these ingrained gifts allowed Ms. Francis, as lieutenant-governor of Nova Scotia (2006-2012), to navigate, deftly and elegantly, the Byzantine labyrinths of protocol and parliamentary procedure, and to outmanoeuvre the Machiavellian and re-educate the (unconsciously) racist. Such episodes are recounted frankly, with good humour, and with courtesy for all, but stern rebuke of bumblers, liars, and transgressors.

Then again, nothing less should be—can be—expected from a head-held-high Black woman, a lady of good upbringing and excellent posture, good manners and parade-square poise, good will and pointillist diction, plus that savvy vocabulary issuing *le mot juste* eloquence. Credit her mother, an Antiguan native, Thelma Delores, for Ms. Francis's interest in the right words in the right order, in righteous speech and right conduct, in choosing the right hat to set off the right shoes, in being in the right places at the right time, to be able to lecture on equal rights, campaign for human rights, and never ever look like she didn't have the right stuff to do the right thing. Maybe Ms. Francis learned also from her mother the efficacy of feminism—or Afro-womanism—to never let the masculine denigrate or degrade, deride or deprive. Thus, she possesses the smarts and the drive to conjoin know-how and ethics to can-do and work-ethic; to progress, to move-on-up, to be an X-ray technician here and a paralegal there, a runway model in Manhattan and a role-model in Nova Scotia, a CEO in public life and a churchgoer in private life. But she's also acquired those essential Black woman complements: to "cut eye" at anyone who must be cut down to size; to tongue lash the obstreperously insolent and the self-righteous hypocrite; to espy faults and speak unstopped truth. She be indomitable, charismatic, glamorous, queenly in and of herself: just like mom.

Note that Ms. Francis's memoir is steeped in the magical. Her parents married on Valentine's Day, 1939. She was born at home (during what is now African Heritage Month) in 1946, delivered by a Black doctor who must have been one of the first to open an office in Cape Breton. Her background was immediately multicultural: American, Antiguan, and Cuban; anglophone and Hispanic;

African Orthodox and Episcopalian. Her maturation in the household at 19 Hankard Street, Whitney Pier, Sydney, Nova Scotia, prepared her entrée to the prestigious addresses of the PMO (Prime Minister's Office, Ottawa), Province House and Government House (Halifax), Wall Street skyscrapers (NYC), and, of course, Buckingham Palace. (But it also readied her to accept the embrace of our slave ancestors who haunt Elmina Castle in Accra, Ghana, still wanting to help us understand the tribulation of the Slave Trade and the torture of the Middle Passage.) Elizabeth, her middle name, was chosen in homage to the then-Princess Elizabeth (now *La reine* Elizabeth). What an auspicious foreshadowing of their later connection! In her girlhood, Ms. Francis saw her father integrate—and affiliate socio-politically—with "priests, rabbis, and ministers"; she overheard white parents begging him to intercede in their daughters' love affairs with Black youths—and he did so, but still presided over interracial marriages, anyway. So Ms. Francis learned the facts of Canuck cosmopolitanism in her very household. Outside her doors, there were Jewish merchants and Dutch schoolmates, plus West Indian strivers and achievers. If an ignoramus called her "out her name," someone prestigious called her gifted. So distinguished and well thought of was her family that when Ms. Francis needed resources beyond their means to attend college and university, a Scottish benefactor donated the necessary finances on condition of their acceptance of his eternal anonymity. The *bon mot* that "when one door closes, God opens another" is so applicable in the case of Ms. Francis that the proverbial door may as well be a revolving one. Seldom is she "between jobs." More often, she is about to begin—or has just begun—one technical or managerial or bureaucratic position when the phone rings and she finds herself tapped to take up a higher calling, a more demanding and high-pressure post; to become the lieutenant-governor; to answer to a deputy minister and then be a deputy head; to swear in the premier, the most powerful person in provincial government.

Her ascension is similar to that of Mary Poppins gliding up the banister, except that the gravitational forces arrayed against Ms. Francis were (and are) far greater than what the fictitious Ms. Poppins ever gets to experience. Ms. Francis's *Good Luck* is always a product, first, of her *Pluck*—in acquiring requisite skills or knowledge—then being willing to be challenged in the application. Before she gets to curtsy to the Queen, there's a lot of coffee, a lot of phone calls, a lot of late nights and early mornings, a lot of wear-and-tear on shoe heels and car tires, a lot of subway tokens and airplane tickets. If she's had a charmed existence, it's partly because she's a Christian existentialist—though duly Protestant in work-ethic and archly Catholic in *caritas*.

So, yes, Dr. Francis's story is practically every little girl's dream-come-true: to be Cinderella, and to be elevated from drudgery to governance; to be a princess and reside in a castle. First, she's a Helen Gurley Brown-gal, taking New York by strategy; later, she's the appointed Monarch of the Bluenoses. Malcolm X beamed at her; Harry Belafonte touched her toe. Clearly, both saw they were in the presence of incarnate royalty.

But Her Honour's story is also one of a Black woman's constant struggle to receive the R-E-S-P-E-C-T that Aretha sings of and First Lady Michelle Obama writes about. Her Honour was the Canadian prime minister's vice-regal pick, but one that the Nova Scotian State seemed reluctant to endorse. Ms. Francis found herself in the same Orwellian predicament that beset His Excellency Mr. Obama: to be nominally in power; to be, in fact, empowered; but to be stymied and checkmated by obstructionist politicos and by resolutely reactionary bureaucrats. The 44th—but first Black—President of the United States (2009–2017) got to move into the White House, but found it difficult to move his agenda forward; the 31st—but first Black—Lieutenant-Governor of Nova Scotia, found it difficult to move into Government House, and had to represent the Queen while working out of her cramped condo—for three long years. She also had to tussle with officialdom to try to requisition a proper limo so that she could discharge her constitutional duties and social obligations in something like deputy-majesty style, yes, but also comfort and, above all, safety. In her memoir, Ms. Francis sympathizes with the Obamas and with the 27th—but first Black—governor-general of Canada (2005–2010), Her Excellency Michaëlle Jean, given that all faced resentment from some white folks who could not tolerate their electoral or monarchical-appointment success. Her Honour—Ms. Francis—discovered that some "deplorables" (cf. Ms. Hilary Clinton) would spite protocol by refusing to address her with that primary, legislated moniker. She also found her entrée to her castle— Government House—delayed unreasonably, annoyingly, frustratingly. Indeed, she was kept from residing in the people's-mandated lodging until a new government, of socialist orientation, assumed power and moved expeditiously—not with "all deliberate speed"— to end her *de facto* segregation and/or exile and allow her to reside in the mini-palace intended for every lieutenant-governor since a colonial Nova Scotian governor ordered its construction (utilizing Black slave labour) in 1800. Finally, Her Honour got to "come on home."

Once properly installed in residence, Her Honour, feeling sympathy for and solidarity with Africadian (African-Nova Scotian) businesswoman Viola Desmond, who was jailed in 1946 for disobeying the tartan version of Jim Crow then-operative in a New Glasgow cinema, sought to rectify this racial injustice. On the advice of the new premier, and exercising the Royal Prerogative of Mercy, Ms. Francis issued Ms. Desmond a Free Pardon, the first to ever be granted in Canada, and the first to be granted posthumously. The effect of this majestic act was to nullify Ms. Desmond's original conviction and thus to cancel her original "crime." Not only was she now officially innocent; it was also officially registered that she had done nothing wrong in sitting in the "whites-only" section of the cinema. Thus was *de facto* segregation itself now declared to have been unjust.

One may deem it whimsical that Ms. Francis insisted, when granted her own coat-of-arms, that her beloved feline Angel be depicted at the crown of the heraldic emblem. Yet Her Honour was never, and is not, capricious. Indeed, the scriptural passages that front each chapter of her extraordinary and compelling story clarify that her direction, her course, has been set by moral conviction and a profound appreciation for being humane (including extending love and care to cats) and for the pursuit of justice. She has Christ in her heart, Angel on her crest, and the late Africadian radical activist Burnley "Rocky" Jones, O.N.S., as an exemplar. I love that Her Honour closes her memoir with a shout-out to Rocky, allowing that she has answered the question that he raised with her shortly after his induction into the Order of Nova Scotia in 2011: "Has racism raised its ugly head during your tenure?" Her considered reply, being positive, is negative. Still, the general tenor of this insightful and instructive memoir backs Dr. Martin Luther King's aphorism, "The arc of the moral universe is long, but it bends toward justice."

Dr. George Elliott Clarke, O.C., O.N.S., F.R.C.G.S., Ph.D., LLD., etc.
E.J. Pratt Professor of Canadian Literature
University of Toronto

Chapter 1

THE BEGINNING

*We know that God causes everything to work together for
the good of those who love God and are called according
to his purpose for them.*

ROMANS 8:28

"**M**y goodness, I disconnected the prime minister's
office; they wanted to speak to you," said my executive assistant, Michael Noonan.

Laughing I said, "Someone is playing tricks on you."

"No, I am serious," he said, sounding panicky. "I have to call
them back."

Little did I know that phone call would change forever not only
the course of my life, but the history of Nova Scotia.

Who would have thought or imagined that I, a Black woman,
born of immigrant parents and raised in a province with a history of negative race relations and racial segregation would be
receiving a call from the Prime Minister of Canada asking me

to accept a position that would prove to be a great blessing, a very rewarding experience, even though there were times it was challenging.

IN RETROSPECT, the foundation for my successful journey was there very early in my life. I believe God's plan for my path was laid out before I came into this world. I was born in Sydney, Nova Scotia, in a community called Whitney Pier on Cape Breton Island, three years after my sister Isabel, and three months after Viola Desmond, a Black businesswoman, was arrested on November 8, 1946, and later convicted, for sitting in a whites-only section in a movie theatre in New Glasgow, Nova Scotia. Who could have guessed that my life and Ms. Desmond's would merge in 2010?

My parents were immigrants. My father, Archpriest George Anthony Francis, and my mother, Thelma Delores Francis, came to Sydney in 1940, the year after they were married. My father was born Jorge Antonio Francisco Francis Y Edivardis in Santiago de Cuba on February 16, 1908. According to Spanish custom my father had two last names, Francis and Edivardis. The father's name is first, followed by the mother's name. Since women did not change their last names when they married, it proved

Mayann Francis's paternal grandfather, Jacobo Francis Fedriche. (COURTESY OF AUTHOR)

Mayann Francis's father, George Anthony Francis, as a young man. (COURTESY OF AUTHOR)

to be a valuable way to trace one's ancestry. The father's name, which in this case is Francis, is passed on to the children. His parents, Jacobo Francis Fedriche (Fedriche would be his mother's name) and Ana Maria Edivardis, were born in Antigua, which was at that time an English colony. They immigrated to Cuba where my grandfather, who spoke fluent Spanish, worked as a bricklayer. Being bilingual endeared my grandfather to his new community, and he was highly respected. He was a member of the Masonic order called the Odd Fellows. I know very little else about my maternal and paternal grandparents.

My father, along with his sister Maria and brother Eduardo, left Cuba in 1929 for New York City. After a series of jobs, he decided to study for the ministry and became an ordained priest in the African Orthodox Church. The African Orthodox Church was founded in Chicago in 1921 by George Alexander McGuire, who left the Episcopal Church where he was studying because he experienced racism as a Black deacon. He also established, in 1922, the now-defunct Endich Theological Seminary to train African Orthodox

Mayann Francis's siblings, George Anthony and Eloise Yvonne, were raised by Francis's grandmother in Cuba.
(COURTESY OF AUTHOR)

priests, which is where my father studied in New York.

When he married my mother, my father had two children. My father's first wife died at an early age. Together they had George Anthony and Eloise Yvonne, who were five and three, respectively, when their mother died. My father's sister Maria decided to take the children to Cuba to be raised by my grandmother Ana and my father's other sisters, my aunts Olga, Felicia, and Dora, who was the youngest. By this time my grandfather was deceased. George and Eloise remained in Cuba for close to ten years and returned to New York when the remainder of the family immigrated there.

In 1939, on February 14, my dad married my mother in New York City. My father was not a great fan of New York, so a year later, when the opportunity presented itself for him to pastor St. Philip's African Orthodox Church in Sydney, Nova Scotia, he answered the call. George and Eloise remained in New York. Even after all these years, I still wish that my siblings had been raised in Canada with Isabel and me. I often wonder why it wasn't that way. It is a secret the family has taken to their graves. My aunts were very hardworking and strong women. Somehow, I do not think my father would have petitioned them for his children to live with us in Canada. As close as I was to my siblings, we never discussed why we were raised in different countries. I did, however, ask my mother about this. Her only answer was, "That's the way your aunts wanted it."

Even though my brother and sister were raised in Cuba and Brooklyn, New York, the distance between us did not negatively impact the relationship I had with

Mayann Francis's paternal grandmother, Ana Maria Edivardis. (COURTESY OF AUTHOR)

them. Every second summer, my parents, Isabel, and I would travel by train from Cape Breton to New York to visit family. Eloise called me "Freshie." She told me that when I was a child, I was quick to speak my mind. She said I had a way of looking at someone, closing my eyes, and looking away. She referred to this as "cutting your eyes" at someone. In her opinion this was rude. We often laugh about this because she says I still have that look when someone does not please me.

George died in December 2014. He was a special brother and I miss him. He never failed to tell anyone whom he came in contact with about his little sister, the lieutenant-governor. Eloise still lives in New York. We became very close during the years I lived there. She is my buddy. When I was studying for my master's in public administration, I attended night classes at New York University. I would often stay with Eloise and her husband because travelling alone at night back to Brooklyn where I was living was not wise. Whenever I wanted to go partying, Eloise, as tired as she was, would go with me. We always had fun. Or I should say, I always had a blast! Her husband, Morris, and I loved to tease my sister. Morris died on May 28, 2007, two days before I first met Her Majesty Queen Elizabeth II in Buckingham Palace. I was at the Halifax airport waiting to board my flight to London when I received the news of his death.

Eloise was and still is one of the greatest cooks I have ever known. This skill she inherited from our father and the aunts. She was a nutritionist. I can still remember her going to university at night, working during the day, taking care of her home, and staying up to the wee hours of the morning working on her school projects. I admired her determination. She graduated with her master's from New York University. Years later, I would also graduate from the same university, prompted by her example and encouragement.

My mother, Thelma Delores, was born in Antigua on October 20, 1907. She left the West Indies for New York City when she was in her late teens. Her life in Antigua was from all accounts a sad one. My mother was a beautiful woman. People referred to her as the quintessential lady. Mother loved music. To hear her sing "O Holy Night" was so moving. She had a voice like her idol Marian Anderson, a famous contralto of the twentieth century who in 1955 was the first African American to perform with the New York Metropolitan Opera.

In her later years my mother suffered from dementia. It was difficult to watch her sink into a world where we could not reach her. When we played tapes of opera singers like Marian Anderson, and hymns or gospel music, a smile would come across her face. It was beautiful to witness this brief transformation. She died on December 3, 2000, at the age of ninety-three.

At my mother's funeral I described her as a proud woman who walked with her head held high. Whenever she wore her chapeau, white gloves, and high heels, heads turned, people smiled, and the men tipped their hats because an African queen was passing by. Here is the tribute to my mother I wrote for the Halifax *Chronicle Herald* on May 26, 2006, "Celebrating Mother, a True Friend."

Mayann Francis's mother, Thelma Delores, was said to be "the quintessential lady." (COURTESY OF AUTHOR)

My mother did not graduate from high school, and the dream of a diploma eluded her for many years. When she immigrated to New York, she worked in factories during the day and earned her high school certificate while attending school in the evenings.

When I was a child, she achieved her practical nursing certificate through a correspondence course. She treated the certificate like it was made out of gold. It was one of her most precious treasures. Her excitement made me proud. It taught me something about the worth of education, and it is a lesson I have carried with me throughout my journey. I laugh every time I think about the time I came home from school and told my mother I was going to quit school at the age of sixteen because school was too lonely and nothing related to me as a young Black girl. "Not under my roof," was her reply. I will never forget the look of horror in her eyes. "Hold your head high and walk proud, because you can be somebody. You will stay in school. Life is about learning and having dignity and being proud of who you are." Her words have guided me every step of my life.

In school, as Black children, we did not learn about Black history or about Black heroes. Because of this omission by the

educational system, my mother, with her limited education,
would talk about Black success stories. These included people
like Ralph Bunche, an accomplished African American academic
and United Nations diplomat, Mahalia Jackson, a famous gospel
singer, Marian Anderson, and many others. She wanted us to
know that we could be who we wanted to be and education was
too important and precious to be taken lightly.

My mother was not perfect. Her cooking skills were not the best. My father made breakfast for my sister and me. He usually made bologna, eggs, toast, and hot chocolate. We were not so happy when our mother made breakfast. Eating porridge was not as exciting as eating fried eggs and bologna.

My maternal grandmother's name was Louisa Wilson. From all accounts she was a very beautiful woman. Mother didn't discuss her early life very much, and when asked, she would only give bits and pieces. My mother had two sisters and one brother. Her mother never married. Even though my grandmother was a single woman with four children, she was fully accepted in the community. Louisa Wilson was Creole, of mixed blood—Black, white, and Indian. She had long straight black hair. Both my mother and her brother were of dark complexion, and her sisters looked like my grandmother. I asked my mother if she knew her father. Her only recollection was of a tall dark man coming to visit. She said she called him "Pa." His name was Henry George. I tried to trace the lineage but hit a brick wall.

One day my mother told me a story that brought tears to my eyes. I cannot imagine the pain she must have felt then and probably felt for the rest of her life. She and her brother were playing in the backyard of their home on Dickenson Bay Street in St. John's, Antigua. A white man, who may have been a missionary because he was holding a book that my mother thought was a Bible, came into the yard. He noticed the children and asked who the pretty little girl was. According to my mother, her mother told the man that she belonged to a neighbour.

I do not know if my grandmother considered herself a Black woman (or for that time period, a Negro). My mom's story led me to wonder if my grandmother would have been proud to be called "Negro" or "coloured." My mother believed that my grandmother favoured mother's two sisters, who had their mom's high-yellow colour and hair texture. Some of my cousins who knew my grandmother confirmed that she did not like people with dark skin. I would have liked to have met her with my dark skin and kinky hair.

Mayann Francis's maternal grandmother, Louisa Wilson. (COURTESY OF AUTHOR)

To understand my grandmother, we have to understand the legacy of slavery. My grandmother is an example of the negative psychological impact of slavery, colonization, and internalized racism. Light skin and straight hair are closer to being white, and there was the mistaken belief that someone with these features would be fully accepted by the white race and granted privileges. Fortunately this attitude has changed over the years. We see many Black women of various colours and hair texture on the big screen and on television, thanks to Black women writers and producers like Shonda Rhimes. Her television shows *How to Get Away with Murder* and *Grey's Anatomy* are excellent examples of this. Nonetheless, there are still some Black people who have unfortunately internalized the negative attitude about Black women perpetuated by slavery and make stupid comments about "good" (i.e., straight) hair and "bad" (i.e., curly or kinky) hair. Black women, be proud of who you are regardless of your skin colour or hair texture.

In her late teens my mother left Antigua for the United States. She never returned there until after the death of her mother decades later. Neither my mom nor her brother attended their mother's funeral. Now I understand why. My grandmother, I believe, was in her late eighties when she died. My mother did provide for her, often sending her money.

Little is known about my mother's time in New York. I know she lived with her godmother who sponsored her to the United States. My parents took my sister and me to visit Mother's godmother, whom we called Granny. I remember her as a tall, thin, dark-skinned woman with grey hair on her head and chin. I used to stare at her chin. I wanted to reach up and pull the hairs out. She always fed us white rice whenever we went to visit. My sister and I would cringe when she dished out our portion of rice, which resembled a bowl of white paste. Our parents left us no choice but to eat it. For them it was about respect and being grateful for the food placed in front of us. When I became an adult I did not eat white rice for many years.

How parents met in New York, I do not know. The bits and pieces I managed to extract from my mother do not fill in the blanks. I do know that her life in New York was hard, but she also had fun. She worked in factories, studied at night, cleaned her godmother's place, and sent money back to Antigua.

When my father decided to move to Nova Scotia in 1940, my mother, from what I understand, was not keen. She didn't want to move to a place that she thought was the end of the Earth. Can you imagine leaving New York after experiencing and taking part in the excitement of the Harlem Renaissance?

My mother's arrival in Cape Breton months after my father's arrival was very dramatic. When she purchased her train ticket in New York, the clerk sold her a ticket to North Sydney instead of Sydney. She arrived in North Sydney during a snowstorm. Meanwhile my father was waiting at the Sydney train station, twenty-two kilometres away. Imagine his face when my mother did not disembark! My mother was sitting in North Sydney, crying and afraid. She truly believed she had arrived at the end of the Earth. She was unaware that my father and Mr. Horton Murray, a Whitney Pier taxi driver and a member of my father's congregation, were driving through a snowstorm to get her. Apparently, the railroad clerk had noticed her crying and called the Sydney station as soon as he realized that she was supposed to disembark there.

My parents began their married life at 19 Hankard Street, Whitney Pier, the house where I was born. As a child I thought the house was big, but it was a very small two-storey house, with three bedrooms and a bathroom upstairs. Isabel and I shared one bedroom, and Mom and Dad had theirs. It was common in our community that siblings shared a bedroom, regardless of the size of the room. The other bedroom was considered a guest room. The kitchen was where we ate our family meals. There was no dining room. When I delivered a presentation to students about my life as a child and showed them pictures of the house where I was raised, I overheard a young boy say, "That's a shack."

I was born at home. Dr. Calder, a Black doctor, brought me into this world. He was from the Caribbean and lived "over town." Nurse Dobin, a white nurse, assisted in the delivery. Dr. Calder is also credited with saving my life. My mother told me that I developed pneumonia during a bout with the measles and almost died. Dr. Calder rushed me to the hospital and started immediate treatment. I dreamt that I was surrounded by plastic. I later found out it wasn't a dream—I was in an oxygen tent.

A very young Mayann Francis at her home on Hankard St. in Sydney, Nova Scotia's Whitney Pier.
(COURTESY OF AUTHOR)

My parents decided to name me Mayann Elizabeth. They wanted to satisfy both sides of the family. May was my mother's sister and Ann is the English translation of my father's mother's name. Elizabeth, you guessed correctly, is after Princess Elizabeth, future Queen of England. My sister Isabel's middle name is Victoria, so you can see that my parents' admiration for the royal family was clearly a factor in our names. Is it possible my mother had some premonition that one day her second-born would be the vice-regal representative for Her Majesty? My mother and father were privileged to meet Princess Elizabeth and Philip, Duke of Edinburgh, at the Isle Royale Hotel during the royal visit to Nova Scotia in 1951. I recall how excited they were to have the opportunity to meet the royal couple. The Isle Royale Hotel was located on the corner of the Esplanade and Dorchester Street in Sydney. It was demolished in 1985.

My early memories of growing up in Whitney Pier are good ones. Our family of four grew to a family of seven when my parents fostered three children, identical twins Deborah (Debbie) and Donna Marshall, and Karl (Howard) Francis-Williams. They were each three years old when they came to live with us. I was

Mayann Francis (centre) with her twin foster sisters, Donna (left) and Deborah Marshall. The twins joined the family in 1957. Karl (Howard) Francis-Williams, joined the family later, in 1965.

(COURTESY OF AUTHOR)

eleven when the twins joined our family in 1957. The guest bedroom became theirs. I was excited knowing that I would have two younger siblings. I have vivid memories of their arrival. It was a cold winter day. They both wore blue snowsuits. At first they would not talk. But when they went to their bedroom, we could hear them talking to one another and laughing. The next day, they started talking to us. It was beautiful.

Our family still travelled to New York to visit our relatives. The first time we travelled with the twins, we did not go by train. Instead, we travelled by plane. We all enjoyed our time spent in New York with our American Cuban family.

Isabel and I had already left home when Howard joined our family in 1965. The twins were thirteen years old when he came. Howard took over the guest bedroom and the twins occupied the room vacated by me and my sister. Howard and I both liked to eat and our dad loved to cook. Need I say more? Howard loved our family so much that he legally added Francis to his name. He had a special relationship with our parents. His dedication to them was remarkable. He was always there when they needed him. He often travelled with our parents to New York, Halifax, and Antigua.

We were blessed because all three remained with our parents well into their adult lives. Debbie and Donna, who are both committed to public service, now live in Toronto where their 102-year-old biological mother is also a resident. They are very close to their mother, which I think is wonderful. Their dad died when they were babies. Howard lives in Nova Scotia. Both his biological parents are deceased. We are all still close and often share many laughs and stories about growing up at 19 Hankard Street.

Chapter 2

I AM A PIER DEAR

You are the light of the world—like a city on a hilltop that cannot be hidden. No one lights a lamp and then puts it under a basket. Instead a lamp is placed on a stand, where it gives light to everyone in the house.

MATTHEW 5:14–15

For a moment I could not speak. I was sitting across from the prime minister of our beautiful country, Canada, and he had just asked me to be the thirty-first lieutenant-governor of Nova Scotia. I stared in disbelief while Prime Minister Stephen Harper continued to speak. All I could think about were my parents and all those warriors who fought for equality and justice for Black people. There I was, a Black woman from humble beginnings, sitting with the prime minister, who had selected me to be the vice-regal representative. Not only was I surprised; I was also gripped with fear.

I would be the first Black person to achieve this high honour in Nova Scotia. Would the wider community accept me? I knew the expectation and the challenge in taking on such a role were enormous. I had forty-eight hours to respond. I could not tell anyone. I felt alone.

I was well aware that regardless of my answer my life would be impacted forever. Did I want to throw away this opportunity? After all, my parents taught me to walk proud. And as long as I had my education, I could do anything. Did I want my life to become an open book, as it probably would if I accepted the honour? I had so many questions and no answers. My inner voice said, "Fear should not stop you. When a door opens, it opens for a reason."

I knew what I had to do to arrive at my answer. I spoke to someone I could trust.

WHEN MY parents came to Nova Scotia they did not know what to expect. Nonetheless, they took the plunge into unchartered territory. It was my parents who laid the foundation for the road I would travel in life.

I grew up in a diverse community of immigrants in Whitney Pier. We lived in harmony with the non-Black immigrants, people who had come from different parts of the world in search of employment and a better life for themselves and their children. People left their homes in the Ukraine, Poland, and Lebanon and crossed the oceans to come to Cape Breton. There were Acadians, Jewish people, and West Indians who lived with the descendants of earlier waves of Scottish and Irish immigration. Many immigrants found jobs in the Sydney steel plant. Some were also entrepreneurs. We were a strong, hardworking, and closely knit community.

In the book *From the Pier, Dear! Images of a Multicultural Community* published by the Whitney Pier Historical Society in 1993, Whitney Pier is described as

...a distinct part of Sydney, Nova Scotia, which slopes up from the east side of Sydney Harbour in three successive ridges. It is a triangle-shaped area located on the northeast corner of the city, contained in about three squares miles. The only connection with the rest of Sydney ('over town') is a huge overpass. Yet residents and outsiders alike recognize both the physical and social boundaries of this unique community. Whitney Pier is noted as much for its solidarity as for its diversity. Whitney Pier's sense of place is expressed with staunch pride in being 'from the Pier, dear.'

My father's church, St. Philip's African Orthodox Church, was the only church of its kind in Canada. St. Philip's was established by Reverend William Ernest Robertson in 1921. Members of the Black community at that time were not welcomed in the white Anglican church in Sydney. The West Indian community petitioned the African Orthodox Church in New York City for permission to organize a church where they could feel free to worship in peace. Reverend Robertson served for one year, followed by Reverend Father Trotman (1922–25), Venerable Archdeacon Dixon Egbert Philip (1925–36), Reverend Father James Adolphus Ford (1936–38), and Reverend Father Rafael Jones (1938–40). As you can see, most of these men did not stay in Sydney for longer than two to four years. It was rumoured that they felt the weather was too harsh and the people difficult.

My father was the pastor of St. Philip's African Orthodox Church for over forty years, from 1940 to his death in 1982. He was elevated to canon in 1948 and vicar general in 1970. But Father Francis, as he was called, did not like big titles. He wanted people to call him Father, not Vicar or Canon. Shortly after my father's death, my sister Isabel's husband, Archbishop Vincent Waterman, began his tenure in Sydney. Archbishop Waterman was elevated to the position of Patriarch of the African Orthodox Church in 2015. Sadly, he passed away at the age of ninety-three on January 22, 2019, in Halifax.

Under my father's leadership, St. Philip's became the focal point for the Black community of Whitney Pier. There were numerous churches in "the Pier." It was common for priests, rabbis, and ministers to come together to discuss community matters. I realize now the influence these men had on their respective communities. Many families depended on these religious leaders, not only for spiritual advice—in some cases to settle family disputes and also for social services.

My father met with white business owners in our community and beyond, insisting that they hire Black people. Back then there was no Human Rights Commission, no employment equity or affirmative action programs. Father Francis saw an injustice and was trying to make things right. He would find secretarial and retail jobs for Black women.

When I was sixteen, my father was able to secure a job for me "over town," in the Five and Ten Store during Christmas rush. Even though the job was only for a few weekends, I was very excited. What happened to me there is still vivid in my memory. I was assigned to the checkout where I bagged purchased items. A male customer at another checkout said, "Oh look, a n_ _ _ _ r." No one said anything. Not even me. I did not tell my parents. I buried it deep within me.

This was not the first time I experienced this kind of attitude. I remember an incident when I was in grade six. A white boy said he did not like my friend because her face was black and mine was dirty. And in grade three, we were playing a game during recess that involved holding hands. I could not understand why every time one of the white girls held my hand she would wipe her hand on her clothes. It is amazing how experiences from your early life remain with you. Fifty years later, when we held hands in one of my aerobics classes, I couldn't help but think about my experience in grade three. Thankfully, history did not repeat itself.

Many of the men who had arrived in Whitney Pier from the West Indies brought their trades and entrepreneurial spirit. There was a tailor shop, a barbershop, a watch-repair shop, and a co-op store. Mr. Horton Murray, who was a close friend of our family, operated his own taxi business. (It was Mr. Murray who drove my father to retrieve his wife from the North Sydney train station. He is the taxi driver in my children's book, *Mayann's Train Ride*.) It was a community that emphasized hard work and education. Many worked in the steel plant, often under dangerous conditions. I remember my father being called to break the news to families when their loved ones suffered a fatal accident in the plant. The community was strong and rallied to help those in need, regardless of colour. We were a proud community of immigrants.

In 2011, I along with the Speaker of the Nova Scotia House of Assembly, Gordie Gosse, a resident of Whitney Pier, unveiled a monument in Whitney Pier dedicated to the immigrants who populated the area. The Melting Pot Monument featured twenty-seven flags representing the nations immigrants had left in order to make Whitney Pier their home. Unfortunately, the harsh Nova Scotia weather took a toll on the flags, and work was needed to replace the weather-damaged monument.

We were a community who shared and cared for each other. As soon as my sister and I outgrew our clothes, Mother gave them to families in need. The colour of our neighbours' skin did not matter. All that mattered was that they were in need of clothing. I credit my acceptance of people regardless of their background to growing up in the diverse community of Whitney Pier. My parents played a key role in my outlook and socialization by showing us how to be kind and respectful to people regardless of their colour. My parents' involvement in community and church, as well as growing up in an immigrant community, set the stage for my very public journey.

My father not only gave his time to the church, he was also involved in public service by serving on countless boards: Canadian

Cancer Society, Right to Life, the Canadian Bible Society, the Cape Breton United Appeal (now called the United Way), and many more. An eloquent orator, my father was often in demand as a public speaker. On Sunday mornings, his sermons would shake the church off its foundation. I admired my father's ability to speak in front of large audiences. I knew when I became an adult I wanted to be a public speaker. And I did. Like my dad, I enjoy public speaking.

While in New York every second summer, my father was often the guest preacher at various African Orthodox churches. One of our biannual family trips to New York was the inspiration for my book *Mayann's Train Ride*, a children's story published in 2015. The church where my father preached plays a role in the story. Because he was fond of trains, he organized our church picnics to take place in Boisdale, in the northern part of Cape Breton, and we would travel to the picnic grounds by train.

Our church picnics in Boisdale were so much fun. Many who left Whitney Pier to search for employment in Toronto or elsewhere returned home every year for the church picnics. The night before the big day, households were busy cooking West Indian food to take to the picnic, mostly prepared by the women. Pig's feet, Coo-Coo, peas and rice, fish cakes, fried chicken, black pudding, sugar cake, johnnycake, baked ham, sweet potatoes, and delicious gravy along with the absolutely fabulous hot sauce prepared by Mrs. May Crawford. Our neighbour, Mr. Lambert Bryan, made ginger beer, a non-alcoholic drink that would set your throat on fire. Mom also made sandwiches for the train ride.

One year when it was time to return to Sydney, people did not want to leave. Some stayed behind because they had driven to Boisdale instead of taking the train. Unfortunately, on their way back to Sydney, they had an accident and one of the men, who was an active member of our church and choir, died from his injuries a few days after the crash. This devastated my father and the community. My father did not continue church picnics after that tragedy.

Dad also played a prominent role beyond the Pier community. He made sure that families had sufficient food and decent housing. He spoke Spanish and was often called upon to serve as a translator, especially for seafarers. He settled community disputes as well. White parents from "over town" often visited my father because they did not want their teenage daughters dating Black boys. They pleaded with my father to talk to the boys' parents and put an end to these relationships. He did speak with the parents of the boys to convey what he was told. What happened after that, I do not know. I do know that my father often married interracial couples.

Whenever the altar boys got into trouble, my father would receive a call either from the school or their parents. Their punishment was usually related to church duties like polishing candlesticks or cleaning the church pews.

Law enforcement consulted with my father when someone from the community was in trouble with the law. And politicians often came to our home. I recall my father telling my mom that he hoped the politicians would not forget the community. He knew the importance of voting and encouraged members of the community to follow his example and cast their ballots.

I did not know my mother's first name until I was about ten years old. My parents called one another "hon," short for "honey." It came as a surprise to me when my mother told me that her name was Thelma. She was known as the first lady of the church, where she taught Sunday school. She immersed herself both in the church and community. When my mother went to church, she looked like a fashion queen. She wore her high-heeled shoes, gloves, beautiful dresses, and coats. She always wore a hat to church. Growing up, we had clothes for school, clothes to play in, and Sunday clothes. We did not have much, but our mother believed there was no excuse for not looking clean and tidy. She made many of our clothes. Her views about clothes would impact my views about how to dress later in my life.

Mother shopped at clothing stores in the Pier like Dodicks and Archie Nathanson. I remember my first pair of patent leather shoes from Nathanson's and the beautiful coats and dresses she would buy for my sister and me from Dodicks for Christmas. Mrs. Dodick allowed Mother to buy on credit, and every week I was sent to Mrs. Dodick to put a down payment on the bill. The merchants often allowed members of the community to buy on credit. The Jewish merchants, who themselves had fled persecution in their home countries, had many stores, treated everyone well, and played an active role in the community.

In addition to being a Sunday school teacher, my mother also formed a sewing club for girls. Of course, my sister and I were both in it. After Mother's death, so many women who were in her sewing club remarked how the club impacted their lives. You see, sewing was not the only skill she taught us. We were taught responsibility by paying dues—about twenty-five cents. The dues were for club supplies, which my mother bought. We learned to pay attention to the detail that our projects required. We also had to complete our projects within the timeframe she gave us. The club met in our home every Monday after school. Seldom did anyone miss club. At the end of club we would hold hands and recite one of my favourite prayers, which I later learned is a variant of Genesis 31:49: "Lord watch between me and thee while we are absent one from one another. Thanks for the evening, comrade." With that, club was over for the week.

My mother also chaired the Women's Auxiliary of our church. One evening she was hosting a meeting at our home. It was the same day I had returned home from school crying because one of my classmates had died. I was in grade four. Betty was someone I liked very much. She was from Holland, and her family had been planning a trip back to Holland. The previous week our class had given her a diary so she could write about her vacation and share her stories with us when she returned to Sydney. We were talking and laughing on Friday and by Monday she was dead. To this day I'm uncertain what caused her sudden illness and subsequent death.

In those days the psychological support for such shocking news was your family. When I arrived home, I was distraught because I would never see Betty alive again. Even though my mother was hosting the ladies' auxiliary meeting that evening, she took time to comfort me. She said I could sleep in my parents' bedroom until her meeting was over. When she woke me, I said to her, "I saw Betty. She was wearing her red dress. " I loved that red dress. She often wore it to class. My mom hugged me and smiled. I went to bed thinking about Betty.

The next day we went to Betty's home to pay our respect to Betty's parents and for me to say goodbye to my friend. In the 1950s, deceased people were waked in their homes, not funeral parlours. Betty's family lived on Henry Street, a few streets from where we lived on Hankard. Betty looked like she was sleeping. She was wearing the red dress. I still think about her. I remember her fondly because she was friendly, kind, and she was always smiling. I know she would have been a wonderful person who embraced others regardless of their race or background.

My mother was often described as a lady with poise, grace, and charm. I remember an incident when she used her charm to say no to someone. A man from the community called one night because he wanted my father to come immediately to his home. Apparently, his father was roaming the house, disturbing his sleep. My mother suggested that he ask his father to have a seat for the evening and she would be sure to send Father Francis first thing in the morning. Because the man's father was deceased, my mother felt his request could wait till morning. My father spent time with the man the next day.

Like other members of the West Indian community, my mother greatly valued education. As first-generation Nova Scotians, it was drilled into us that to succeed in life we had to be educated. In fact, the emphasis on education was widespread throughout Whitney Pier, which has resulted in many prominent and successful people in Canada and elsewhere. J. Michael MacDonald became Chief of the Appeals Court of Nova Scotia; Valerie Miller, a lawyer, was elevated to Tax Court Judge; Gordie Gosse was Speaker of the Nova Scotia House of Assembly; Winston Ruck became first Black president of the United Steelworkers Union; Clotilda Yakimchuk, among her many accomplishments, was the first Black president of the Registered Nurses Association—she is also a recipient of the Order of Canada and the Order of Nova Scotia. There are many others who have also achieved success, too many to name. The Pier turned out secretaries, artists, plumbers, doctors, dentists, teachers, and politicians. Consequently, I strongly believe in continuous learning and education. Once you have achieved your education, no one can take it away from you.

I was looking through my mother's papers after her death. I found a scribbler she used when she attended night school in New York. The first entry was dated January 5, 1936. It contained arithmetic problems, Roman numerals, exercises in grammar, and short essays. In later years she used the same scribbler to record events such as the day she and my father met the Right Honourable Georges Vanier, Governor General of Canada, and Madame Vanier at the Isle Royale Hotel in Sydney, on July 14, 1960. She also recorded that on February 15, 1965, the new Canadian flag was hoisted at Parliament Hill in Ottawa. Other entries about current events showed me a side of my mother that I did not know. I often wonder what she might have accomplished if she had been born in another era.

My mother was a stickler for a neat and tidy home. Even though our home was small and certainly not fancy, it was always clean. When I reflect about her cleaning the house, I realize how hard she worked, mopping floors, dusting, cleaning windows, ironing our clothes, cooking, washing dishes, grocery shopping, making clothes for my sister and me, and countless other things. I do not recall my father doing housework. However, whenever he cooked or baked, he left the kitchen clean.

It was many years before we were able to afford a washing machine. My mother wrote in her scribbler that she received her washing machine in June 1960. Prior to this she washed everything by hand on a scrub board in a large tub. When we were old enough, my sister and I learned how to use the scrub board.

Isabel and I were not permitted to sleep in past ten o'clock on a Saturday morning. To do so, in our mother's view, meant you were lazy. We had chores to do. I am sure some people of my generation will remember putting newspapers down on a freshly mopped floor to keep it clean. This was usually my chore. I certainly did not carry this practice into adulthood. I am, however, a morning person. My mother would be proud.

One of the chores I did not like was dusting the woodwork, which meant getting down on my hands and knees and cleaning the wood trimmings, which my mother inspected when I finished. Sometimes, I had to go back and redo areas.

We had pets growing up. Over the course of several years we had dogs and cats. The cats were good mousers. To this day I love cats and I am afraid of mice. I like dogs as well, but I prefer cats. Cats are independent and so am I. I do not have to walk them.

My faith in God has been my foundation from childhood. Sundays were reserved for church and spending time together as a family. At Sunday morning service the church was filled with loud and beautiful singing. Our next door neighbour, Mrs. Susan Bryan, was the organist and did not hesitate to tell the choir to "sing up." I remember fondly the West Indian men and women in the choir and the congregation singing hymns with gusto and passion. My father would announce Hymn 165 (from *Hymns Ancient and Modern*) and the church would erupt in song.

O God, our help in ages past,
Our hope for years to come,
Our shelter from the stormy blast,
And our eternal home;

Beneath the shadow of thy throne,
Thy saints have dwelt secure;
Sufficient is thine Arm alone,
And our defense is sure.

Oh God, our help in ages past,
Our hope for years to come,
Be thou our guard while troubles last,
And our eternal home. Amen.

Our Sunday morning service was what I would describe as high mass. In the evening we had vespers. I loved singing the *Magnificat*, which is found in the Gospel of Luke (1:46–55):

My soul magnifies the Lord, and my spirit rejoices in God, my Saviour, for He has looked with favour on the lowliness of His servant. Surely from now on all generations will call me blessed; for the Mighty One has done great things for me, and holy is His name. His mercy is for those who fear Him from generation to generation. He has shown strength with His arm; He has scattered the proud in the thoughts of their hearts.

The *Magnificat* warms my soul and gives me comfort and peace.

When our family went on holiday to New York, the closing hymn on the last Sunday morning before vacation ("God Be With You Till We Meet Again") was sung very slowly with every word enunciated. It was as if they were dragging heavy bags of coal.

God be with you till we meet again;
By His counsels guide, uphold you,
With His sheep securely fold you:
God be with you till we meet again.

I grew up in the era of the Beatles. One Sunday evening when they were scheduled to appear on *The Ed Sullivan Show*, I begged my dad to conclude service before 8:00 P.M. so we could get home in time to watch. He was not impressed and gave me a lecture about making such a request. Oddly, on the Sunday in question, church ended at 7:50 P.M. We lived across the street from the church so there was plenty of time to arrive home and watch the Beatles on our Admiral black-and-white television. For an hour, our tiny living room was transformed into a movie theatre. Instead of popcorn, my father prepared his delicious hamburgers and french fries. No, not frozen fries. He peeled the potatoes and fried them. Oh, how delicious! And his hamburgers, what can I say? A tastier burger cannot be found. No one knows what his secret was to making a moist and yummy hamburger. Of course, for dessert, we had his delicious yellow pound cake. The ingredients for his scrumptious pound cakes are a secret he took to his grave. He was often seen on Saturday mornings baking and cooking for Sunday dinner. I clearly remember waking up on Saturday morning to the smell of homemade bread, baked chicken, peas and rice, or some other dish he was making. Because of my father's talent for cooking, I grew up thinking that all men knew how to cook. Wow, was I wrong. Some of the men I dated along the way had a difficult time locating the kitchen and understanding its use.

On Christmas Day the altar boys and their friends would visit our home, as was the custom in the neighbourhood. Christmas was a time for visiting your neighbours. I waited anxiously for our doorbell to ring. It was exciting knowing the boys would be coming to visit. I had a crush on one of the guys. My parents would serve them a meal. This was probably not their first meal for the day, although they acted like it was.

Christmas was always a special time. We did not have much, even though it felt like we did. Midnight mass was beautiful. The church was decorated, families were reunited with relatives who had moved away, and my sister and I, along with many others, wore our new clothes to church. Everyone was happy. Christmas is still one of my favourite holidays. I try not to get caught up in the rush and stress of the holiday season. I embrace the birth of my Saviour, Jesus Christ. A time for me to give thanks and reflect on what the birth means to my life.

Being the daughter of a priest was not always easy. My parents were both very much disciplinarians. As the minister's daughters, there were so many restrictions. My mother paid close attention to how my sister and I dressed—nothing revealing could be worn. In her words, we must always dress and act like ladies. We had to sit up straight and walk with our heads held high. Maybe this was training for my future role. Plus, I was the second child, and at times my performance was measured against my sister's, especially in school. Teachers would often say, "Oh, you are Isabel's sister. She was a very good student. We know you will do well." No pressure.

We were told not to bring shame on the family name because we were the priest's daughters. So when I failed grade seven (in those days a teacher could fail you whether it was by a few points, or one subject), I was afraid to go home. To my surprise my parents were very supportive and, like me, were in disbelief. They knew how hard I had worked. I vowed that failure would not happen to me again. Thereafter, I sailed through my education. I kept my vow.

I learned that failure is not always a bad thing. We have to look at it as perhaps a message to do things differently. Maybe it is a wake-up call. We have to have the courage to accept failure, learn from it, and move on to something bigger and better. That's right. Try to turn a negative into something positive. Challenging? You bet. Difficult? Oh yes. In the long run, it is up to you to move on, move up, or stand still.

We were expected to go to school and return home immediately when school was finished. Hanging out with friends was a nonstarter. One day I stopped at a friend's house without permission from my parents. When I finally arrived home, there was no point in lying. One of the neighbours told my parents where I was before I reached home. There were spies everywhere. My parents were not happy with me. I had disobeyed them. "You must always set an example. You are the minister's daughter, and we expect better from you." Talk about guilt. I carried their words into adulthood. There are certain things from my childhood that I cannot forget. I was repeatedly told how I must behave. I could either do the opposite of what my parents expected or do as I was told. I chose the latter, with no regret. Was it difficult? Absolutely. But deep in my heart, I knew they were right.

As a Black woman, the barriers of racism and discrimination dictated that I had to break down the stereotype, the low expectations of me. So my behaviour, my attitude, my education, my determination, my dress, my speech, my confidence, and my values had to surpass white people's expectations. That was my parents' iron rule, and although at times harsh, I now fully understand their actions and outlook.

Isabel and I were not allowed to go to dances, but when I was sixteen I managed to convince them that I should be allowed to attend some. My sister was not so lucky. By this time she was in training to be a nurse. I had a knack for getting what I wanted from my dad. As you know by now, he loved to cook, and I enjoyed eating. I would hang around the kitchen when he was baking his apple pie or delicious cake. It did not matter what he was cooking, I wanted to be the tester. My mother knew what I was up to and always chased me away. But Dad and I had a bond. After Mom left, I would sneak back into the kitchen and sure enough, he had a care package for me. Sometimes I ate so fast that I almost choked. I certainly did not want my mother to catch me.

Even though my upbringing was strict, I did have fun. We played games with our neighbours like hopscotch and jump rope, kick the can, marbles, tiddly, tag, baseball, and make-believe school. Recently a male friend and I were musing about growing up in Whitney Pier. He said, "Girl, we had fun but we also were not allowed to disobey our folks." He said he hated it at the time but when he left home to be on his own, he understood why his parents had been strict. Their lessons served us well.

When my parents did not want us to hear what was happening in the community, they would close their bedroom door and whisper. Of course, I would eavesdrop. I know, I know, not nice. But I was curious. Well no, I was nosy.

I heard them talking about "the field" and things that were taking place there. I found out later that the field was the poor man's bedroom. After all, who could afford to take their mistress or lover to a hotel? There was a field behind our house and at the end of our street. Years later a friend told me that he remembered walking home through the field one night and stumbling over something. When he looked, he realized he had stumbled over two bodies. He knew they were alive because the blanket was a-rockin' and a-rollin'.

Our vacations in New York were exciting. I loved the opportunity to spend time with my Cuban American family. Plus it was always such a pleasant experience to see Black professionals. It gave me a sense of comfort and hope to see people who looked like me working in the media, in stores and banks. They were everywhere. Unfortunately, I could not say the same for Nova Scotia. My sister and I both received our first Black doll while we were visiting our family. I named my doll Brenda. She was so beautiful.

I am grateful to have made those trips to New York at such a young age. If it were not for my parents, our trips to New York, the church, and the experiences I had growing up in an immigrant community, I am uncertain what path I would have followed. The

Young Mayann Francis (left) and a friend play in the backyard of her home in Sydney's Whitney Pier. Francis had a Black doll given to her by her parents while they were visiting Cuban American relatives in New York.
(COURTESY OF AUTHOR)

emphasis was always on education and hard work. Growing up in a diverse immigrant community was an advantage because I learned to communicate and compete against people who did not look like me, and I knew I could.

There were challenges. I remember very clearly the behaviour of certain elementary school teachers. Before proceeding to class, we formed a line in pairs, in the morning and after recess. For some reason, my girlfriend and I were never placed at the head of the line. We were the only Black students in this particular class. Being at the front of the line would have meant that my girlfriend and I would lead the students up the stairs to class. We would have been leaders for a few minutes, but we never got the opportunity.

I was a good reader. I always practised reading with my father. I loved reading and I still do. At school there were three reading levels, but I was never placed at the top level. Were these experiences based on race? I do not know. It certainly did nothing for my confidence when I watched little white kids being put at the front of the line or watched them reach the top reading level.

My grade five teacher, who was also my principal, made a positive impression on me. I had poor eyesight and needed to wear glasses, but I refused to wear them for fear of being teased. Sheldon MacDonald noticed me squinting and called me to his desk. He showed me his glasses and said how important it was for me to wear my glasses and not to worry about other people. He took the time to talk to me. He cared. Mr. MacDonald has followed my career. I am still in touch with him and his wife, Carolyn. He was an inspiration.

I was at my father's side when he died, on June 13, 1982. He was there when I took my first breath and I was there when he took his last. Five years before his death he had been diagnosed with prostate cancer. He died at home surrounded by family, members from the congregation, and his doctor. My mother had stepped out of the bedroom for a few seconds when my father took his last breath. When she returned the doctor told her that her husband was dead. She cupped my father's face and asked, "How can you leave me?" My mother never really recovered. Even though she lived until age ninety-three, she was never the same.

Both of my parents were amazing.

AFTER MY meeting with the Prime Minister, I returned to my hotel. I was, I think, in shock. I was alone and I was afraid. I cried. How could I take on this responsibility? What about the people of Nova Scotia? Would they accept a Black woman as their lieutenant-governor?

I was mindful of some of the negative comments Michaëlle Jean received when she was named the first Black governor general. I did not want my family or me to endure a public beating in the press. Michaëlle Jean proved the naysayers wrong. In my opinion, and in the view of many other Canadians, she was an excellent governor general.

To help me make my decision, I relied on my faith; I knew it would steer me in the right direction. Before I went to bed, I confided in Mary, and through her I also talked to God.

"Hail Mary full of grace..."

Next morning, I knew I would be the thirty-first lieutenant-governor of Nova Scotia.

Chapter 3

LEAVING THE PIER

We put our help in the Lord; He is our protector and our help. We are glad because of Him: We trust in His holy name.

PSALM 33:20–21

As the years flew by, my sister and I were busy with our education. Isabel attended Whitney School for junior high, then Holy Redeemer up to grade eleven, and Holy Angels for grade twelve. The latter was "over town." After high school my sister studied to become a nurse at St. Rita's Hospital, which was located on King's Road. (St. Rita's closed in 1995; the hospital in Sydney is now Cape Breton Regional Hospital.) I was glad when my sister stayed in the nurses' residence on Kings Road because I had our small bedroom for myself. Isabel moved to New York shortly after she graduated from nursing school. Our parents were not concerned because our aunts, uncles, brother, and sister were living in New York, where my sister subsequently had a successful career as a psychiatric nurse.

An early school photo of Mayann Francis. She attended Whitney School up to grade seven, then transferred to Don Bosco for the remainder of junior high. (COURTESY OF AUTHOR)

I also attended Whitney School but only up to grade seven. After I failed grade seven, my parents transferred me to Don Bosco, a Catholic school, which was directly behind Whitney School. There I did exceptionally well. I was in the top five when I finished junior high.

I attended Holy Redeemer for grades ten and eleven. I have fond memories of Holy Redeemer. The nuns were strict, but they took a keen interest in us. They encouraged me to excel. I was a member of the school choir. We had Christmas concerts and we even sang on television during the Christmas season. It was great fun. From Holy Redeemer, I went straight into first-year college at Xavier Junior College on George Street, "over town." It was opened in 1951 as a satellite campus of St. Francis Xavier University in Antigonish, Nova Scotia. While I enjoyed college, I wish I had followed in my sister's footsteps and attended Holy Angels. I would have liked the experience of wearing a uniform and continuing at an all-girls' school. Debbie and Donna also attended Holy Angels, and the three sisters often speak fondly about their time there.

When I completed my first year at Xavier, I decided to study X-ray technology. This meant I would have to leave home. This frightened me. I would no longer have the security of my community of Whitney Pier and my family. Halifax would be my home. When I was accepted for studies at the Halifax Infirmary on Queen Street, I was both excited and nervous. My mother was sad to see me leave, but she always believed that education was important. My father took me to Halifax where I would begin my studies. I lived with the Sisters of Service (SOS), who had been operating a women's residence since 1925. My residence at 5206 Tobin Street was opened in 1941 and closed in 1991.

Living at SOS was a wonderful experience. For the first time I had to share a room with girls other than my sister. I met many wonderful girls there, some of whom I maintained contact with long after we went our separate ways. When I was lieutenant-governor, I held a luncheon for some of the women who lived at the SOS residence. It was a lovely and exciting reunion.

I knew my life would never be the same once I left home. My folks looked at this as an opportunity to see if what they had taught me would help me manage on my own. I found my studies challenging. I was thrown into the world of science, which I liked but found intimidating. I had done well in chemistry and physics in high school, so I refused to allow my insecurities to take hold. I settled in to do well.

There were so many lessons learned from training as an X-ray technician. I will be forever grateful that I chose this profession. I learned the meaning of confidentiality, patient privacy, and responsibility and understood the importance of always placing the patient's needs above your own. I X-rayed adults, children, and young adults, and sometimes their diagnosis was terminal. This was difficult. I learned to value life and to demonstrate compassion very early in my life.

I enjoyed working in the hospital because I felt I was making a difference in peoples' lives. I know my role was small, but I felt this was where God wanted me to be at that point in my life. At the time,

Mayann Francis graduated from the X-ray technology program at the Halifax Infirmary in 1966. (COURTESY OF AUTHOR)

I did not know that it was only the beginning of a long, varied career.

Halifax was a very interesting place in the 1960s. My circle of friends was small. My mother's nephew from Antigua was studying commerce at Dalhousie University, and I was happy he was living in Halifax. He, along with a couple of other guys from the Caribbean, lived on Walnut Street. This is where I spent my Sundays. The guys would frequently cook a delicious West Indian meal.

Of course, I knew when parties were taking place. One summer, I went to a party every weekend. The students from Dalhousie always had nice parties, which never got out of control. Many of them were medical, science, engineering, or dentistry students.

One of my disappointments in love was an engineering student. There were other disappointments, but this one stood out more than the others. At the same time he was dating me, unknown to me he was also dating someone else. I stayed strong; I did not want sympathy. My girlfriends rallied around me. I refused to allow his infidelity to break my spirit. I moved on. This was not going to be a burden to weigh me down. I kept my head held so high that I swear I touched the sky a few times. One lesson that has carried me through my life's journey is that when someone disappoints you in love, shed some tears, accept it, and move on and move up. Why let someone break your spirit? Little did I know that this heartbreak would be the first of a few.

I also lived on Victoria Road in Halifax at a boarding house for women. This time I had my own room but shared a kitchen and bathroom. It was a great place to live. The owners were very nice and ran a clean and respectful place. It was one of the few places in Halifax that did not discriminate in their rental practices because of skin colour.

Trying to find a place to live in Halifax was difficult because many owners would not rent to Black people. Apartments were advertised in the newspapers. When you called to inquire about the advertisement and set an appointment, all was well—until you showed up. Then suddenly the place was no longer available, even though it was still advertised in the newspaper the next several days. It was a very frustrating and disturbing experience, a practice I would tackle many years later when I became a human rights officer.

While living at the rooming house, I witnessed for the first time physical assault on a woman. We were allowed to have our boyfriends visit us. My friends and I would often make dinner for our boyfriends and their friends. One evening, my girlfriend and I were watching television when we heard yelling and crying. We went into the hallway then downstairs to the first floor. We knocked at the door where the noise was coming from and to our surprise a man yelled at us to get away from the door. He then chased us back upstairs. We ran back to my room. We were so afraid, we did not know what to do. It was horrible. Shortly after we ran upstairs, things became quiet. The next day, it was clear from the marks on our housemate's face that her boyfriend had hit her.

On another occasion I saw a friend's boyfriend slap her at a party. Years later, I would work on violence against women in my work on social justice issues. Unfortunately, violence against women is still as prevalent today as it was over forty years ago.

All of the parties I attended were West Indian or African, and most of the attendees were university students. New Year's Eve was the height of the parties. Everyone partied at the home of Mary and Moe, two wonderful people who opened their home to students from the Caribbean. Moe was from Trinidad. After Moe's death Mary went on to establish a successful business in Halifax called Mary's Bread Basket.

Even though I enjoyed my time working as an X-ray technician, I had a burning desire to attend university. When I was in grade eleven, one of my teachers, Mother St. Bernard, predicted that I would not remain an X-ray technician. I guess she knew me better than I knew myself. I discussed the possibility of applying to university with my parents. I lacked self-confidence. I was afraid I was not smart enough for university. If I was accepted, would I find a job when I graduated? After all, I was employed as an X-ray technician and I would have to give up my job. How would I pay for my university? What about my rent? I thought of every barrier possible to feed my fears. My parents were supportive. My father told me not to worry about the money, somehow everything would work out.

When I was accepted into Saint Mary's University in Halifax, I was extremely happy. I called my parents to give them the news. I asked how I was going to pay for university. My father laughed. I did not understand why he thought my concern was something to laugh about. He said, "Daughter, I told you not to worry. Things will work out. Go do what you need to do, because you have a guardian angel."

My guardian angel was a Scottish gentleman. It came about through a chance conversation he had with my father about education. The only stipulation attached to his support for my education was that his name must never be revealed. To this day, I have kept that promise. I did manage recently to locate his son, who was aware of his dad's philanthropy and good deeds. I was not the only student he helped. He said his dad helped many people and he never wanted his name revealed. He wanted the recipients to pay it forward.

While I enjoyed university, I also found it intimidating. I did not live on campus, which perhaps added to my feeling of isolation and nervousness. One day while I was changing class, a guy was running down the steps while I was running up. He crashed into me, almost knocking me off my feet.

"Wow," he said.

"I am sorry," I said and kept moving.

In 1973, a few years after that chance meeting, we were married. He was an American from New Jersey and Philadelphia, and I was the small-town girl from Whitney Pier. After our collision on the stairs, he searched the campus until he found me. After all, it was not that difficult. There was only a small number of Black female students on campus, I would say less then twenty.

We had an interesting courtship. Our values were not in sync. This should have been my signal to move on. My faith and religious beliefs were important to me; he did not share them. He did not want to get married in a church, so we married on my girlfriend's lawn in Sackville, Nova Scotia. We wore African outfits because he did not want us to conform to society's view of a traditional wedding. My father performed the ceremony. During our short marriage, many of our arguments centred on religion, oppression, discrimination, and what he would refer to as "the man" who was responsible for racism and discrimination. Even though our marriage failed, I held no anger toward him. He was a nice person, but as long as our values did not line up, our marriage was doomed to fail, and it did. The warning signs were there; we chose to ignore them. At the time of our marriage breakup, we were living in Philadelphia. We tried to reconcile—each time it would end in an argument. I made the decision to move on, and our divorce was finalized in 1980. When I returned to Halifax in the late 1990s, I learned he had died. When we went our separate ways, my wish for him was to find happiness and have a long life. I hope he found the former.

After graduating from Saint Mary's University in 1972, three and half years after I started, I was fortunate to secure a position with the Nova Scotia Human Rights Commission, and was very honoured to receive their Silver Plaque Award in 1974 for outstanding contribution in the field of human rights. When I joined the commission, the executive director was George McCurdy, a truly great leader in Nova Scotia for the fight against racism and discrimination. Mr. McCurdy advocated for equal rights. He was not afraid to challenge the system and met frequently with business and government leaders. I had first come to Mr. McCurdy's attention when as a student I worked on textbook analysis, a summer project for the commission. He was impressed with my work and offered me employment when I completed my degree.

At the commission, we set up many test cases to uncover discrimination in accommodation. It was never difficult to uncover violations of the human rights code. We would have someone Black call about an apartment advertised for rent and set up an appointment within an hour of speaking with the renter. When the Black person went to see the apartment, they were told it had just been rented. We would then have a white person place a call the same day, set an appointment, and visit the apartment. They would be shown and offered the apartment. There was no mention of the apartment no longer being available.

Halifax was a very disturbing place in the 1960s and 1970s. Racism and discrimination were alive and well. It was in the 1960s that Black people were removed from their community of Africville and their homes and church confiscated and demolished to make way for other developments. There was either overt in-your-face racism, or covert racism embedded into systems, policies, and practices

In 2011, Mayann Francis awarded lawyer and activist Burnley Rocky Jones the Order of Nova Scotia. (PROVINCE OF NOVA SCOTIA)

that on the surface seemed neutral but which in reality negatively impacted African Nova Scotians, First Nations, and other racial minorities. Racism and inequality were so prevalent that Halifax was visited by Stokely Carmichael, leader of the Black Panther Party in the United States. The late Rocky Jones, in his book *Revolutionary,* details the visit of Stokely and the Panthers and the state of race relations in Nova Scotia.

Rocky fought for equality. He was not afraid to stand up for what was right. He took to the streets, he yelled freedom, knew when to stand and fight for the right to come in from the margins and into the centre to fight for justice. He was a warrior.

In 2011, I awarded Burnley Rocky Jones the Order of Nova Scotia, the highest honour to be bestowed on a Nova Scotian. Before my tenure as lieutenant-governor ended in 2012, I invited Rocky and his wife, Sharon, for afternoon tea in Government House. I will always remember the look on his face—one of contentment and happiness. This was a man who fought all his life for equity and justice. Seeing me, the first Black vice-regal representative in Nova Scotia, hosting him in this stately home, put a smile on his face that cannot be described. He was proud because he knew that his fight was not in vain. After all, we were sitting in a house that our ancestors, who were slaves, helped to build.

I watched Rocky slowly looking around the room. No longer smiling, he looked at me and in true Rocky style asked whether racism had raised its ugly head during my tenure. I was not surprised by his question. I did not give him a direct answer. We continued to talk.

Interestingly, I found an entry in my journal after a difficult meeting with a politician and a bureaucrat while I was serving as lieutenant-governor. I wrote, "I only ask God to give me the wisdom and health to write my story when this is all over."

My story will answer Rocky's question. Unfortunately, he left this world too soon. He passed away in 2013.

They existed. They existed.
We can be. Be and be
better. For they existed.
- FROM MAYA ANGELOU, "WHEN GREAT TREES FALL"

Chapter 4

TAKING A BITE OUT OF THE BIG APPLE

*No, dear brothers and sisters, I have not achieved it, but
I focus on this one thing: forgetting the past and looking
forward to what lies ahead.*

Philippians 3:13

Life is like a book: there are lessons to learn in every chapter. How we approach the next chapter or next stage in our life depends on what we previously learned. We can become excited, happy, and open to whatever the next chapter of life reveals. Or we can be afraid because we are anxious about the unknown.

After my separation and divorce, I wasn't sure what the book of life had in store for me. I was not approaching the next chapter with excitement. I was scared. I was a single woman with a disability.

While I was working in Halifax as a human rights officer, I noticed how frequently I would trip over objects and bump into things. I drove a blue Gremlin at the time. One afternoon, when I was parking the car in my parking lot, I hooked my fender onto the fender of a truck parked next to me. A few weeks later, I walked into a pole. I had a series of eye tests. When several doctors come into the examining room to talk to you, you know the test results are not good. "Is there anyone in your family who is blind—mother, father, sibling? When did you notice you were bumping into things?"

I was diagnosed with retinitis pigmentosa (RP), a disease of the retina that eventually leads to tunnel vision. I was told that I would gradually lose my eyesight. Doctors in Philadelphia and New York confirmed the diagnosis. The former were blunt and gave me a timeline for when they believed I would lose my central vision. The New York specialist gave me hope. He felt that I might outlive the disease with my central vision intact. I would, however, continue to lose my peripheral vision and depth perception.

Thus began my life of not knowing when my central vision would be reduced to tunnel vision. Even though I was afraid, I did not let this diagnosis stop me from moving forward. I had faith that God would use me in whatever way He felt best.

Even though my central vision is strong, as expected I have very limited peripheral vision and extremely limited night vision. To manage my disability, I have to be extremely aware of my surroundings. When I am walking, I usually scan the room and map out a path so I will not bump into anyone or anything. When I chair meetings, I announce at the start of the meeting that I have limited peripheral vision and may not see folks when they raise their hand to speak. I subsequently rely on the vice-chair or secretary to help me call on members to speak in the order hands were raised. I do not go out at night alone, unless the streets are brightly lit, because I cannot see. When I enter a dark room, I panic, not only because I might bump into people and things but because I might trip and fall because of my limited depth perception.

It is very embarrassing when I meet people for the first time and they extend their hand obviously to shake mine, but I fail to extend mine because I cannot see their extended hand. I now try to extend my hand first, or I casually look down to see if their hand is extended. These are the strategies that I set for myself in order to manage my disability going forward. When I lived in Toronto in the mid- to late 1990s, the Canadian National Institute for the Blind (CNIB) trained me in how to use a white cane, used by people who are blind. It was in Ontario that I was declared legally blind.

I MOVED to New York in 1974, after I separated from my husband, to live with Isabel and her family and find a job. My intention was to remain in New York for six months and then return home to Halifax. Six months turned into sixteen years. I have no regrets about staying in the Big Apple for as long as I did; I feel that New York added to my growth in many different ways. I always had pride in who I was, but living in New York heightened my feeling of pride as a Black woman. I wanted to grow and be successful.

Because of the value my parents placed on education, I knew it was important for me to pursue my studies. Studying at American universities gave me an unexpected confidence. Maybe because there were so many other Black students in my class and on campus, I felt comfortable. I always knew that I could accomplish whatever I set my mind to, and seeing so many successful Black people working in a variety of professions added to my confidence. When I was growing up, Nova Scotia certainly did not offer up opportunity for Black people like I witnessed in New York.

I did not know what to expect when I arrived in New York. I was fortunate to have my family, even though some family members felt I should have stayed with my husband and worked things out. Obviously, I did not listen to them.

I knew I had to find a job. Every day I would search the *New York Times* want ads. I sent out countless resumés and received just as many rejection letters. I was in the big leagues now—New York City. My sister and her husband did not exert any pressure on me. Nonetheless, I wanted to work and not be a burden. I made certain I did my share of work around their home. I enjoyed living with them. We had plenty of laughs. I will always be grateful to them for their patience and support.

My first job in New York was selling *TV Guide* at a call centre. I was excited to have found a job in the Big Apple. Even though it was only part-time, I made the best use of the opportunity. We had to log a certain number of calls per shift and we were expected to make sales. Our calls were monitored and we were given feedback on how to improve our sales pitch. We made calls throughout the United States. I found value in this job because I learned how to be an effective communicator and salesperson. I sharpened my listening skills, looking for an opportunity to change a "no thank you" to a sale. I learned throughout my career to find value in and to learn from every job experience. Every job, no matter what it is, can prepare you for other employment opportunities. Even if the experience was a negative one, I always used it as a learning opportunity to be a stronger and wiser person going forward.

My training as an X-ray technician served me well. I was able to find another part-time job taking chest X-rays in a private agency in midtown Manhattan. I enjoyed meeting many different people. Two part-time jobs worked out well—at least I had money for car fare and other necessities. While working these two jobs, I applied to be a human rights officer with the City of New York. I was granted an interview that I felt went well. Bureaucracy is the same wherever you go, long and drawn out. I would not hear from them until almost a year later.

Meanwhile, I left the job selling *TV Guide*. I had asked for a few hours off to attend my young niece's graduation from kindergarten.

I even offered to make up the time. They denied my request. So I quit. My niece was more important.

Friends of our family suggested I try volunteering. I decided to volunteer at Lennox Hill Hospital in the X-ray department. This was the right move. I was helping one of the technicians when the radiologist introduced himself and asked when I had started my employment with the hospital. He was speechless when I told him I was not being paid. Apparently he read X-rays for private clinics and was looking for a trained technician. He offered me the job at two of his clinics. I was thrilled.

One clinic was located in Spanish Harlem, the other in Coney Island. I had to understand and adapt quickly to the culture around me in two new environments. This was not Nova Scotia. It did not take long for word to spread in these communities that there was a new "tech." The secretarial staff came from the community, and I developed a good relationship with them. My patients included drug addicts, numbers runners, seniors, and many others from the respective neighbourhoods. For me, life is about treating people with respect regardless of their circumstance. The patients needed medical services, not my judgment about their lifestyle. One of the young guys who was dependent on hard drugs stayed free of drugs for a few hours one Valentine's Day so that he could bring me a rose. He thanked me for being nice to him. Whenever I receive roses, I think about him and wonder about his life.

While working in these clinics, I was also studying to be a para-legal at Long Island University in Brooklyn. It was not easy working two jobs and studying. I felt the only way I was going to break into the corporate world was to have a certificate from an American university to complement my degree from Saint Mary's University.

Because I was attending school in Brooklyn, I moved from my sister's home in Queens to live with my Aunt Maria in her magnificent brownstone, which really was more limestone-colour. She lived there by herself, except for the occasional person she wanted to help. She was known for taking in African students, many of whom went on to professional careers both in the United States and Africa. She had a very warm heart and opened her home to many people who needed help.

My aunts, Dora, Olga, and Felecia, her husband, Caleb, and son Randy, lived together in their brownstone not too far from Aunt Maria's home. My aunts were very skilled at sewing, embroidering, and weaving. I am fortunate to have some of their needlework and embroidery, works of art they created when they were growing up in Cuba. Uncle Eddie had his own brownstone. An entrepreneur who had a successful plumbing business, my uncle worked long hours seven days a week. I fondly remember my dear uncle, who was always smiling and full of jokes. No matter what my age, he called me "kid."

Living with my aunt was not always easy. Aunt Maria never married. She was set in her ways and beliefs. She was an incredible woman who was not afraid of hard work. She would leave home in the evening and walk to the subway for her job in Manhattan. She held two full-time jobs as a practical nurse. She never complained. I believe she would have continued working well into her eighties had she not been mugged one evening on her way to work.

Like my parents, Aunt Maria placed great value on education. Her wish for me was that I become a lawyer. Obviously, I disappointed her. I will always remember her words when I graduated from New York University with my master's in public administration: "Maybe now, you will go to law school," she said. Wow, talk about not feeling appreciated—her words tore into me like a sharp dagger plunged into my heart.

Maria was a great cook. American Thanksgiving was always held at her home. Sometimes there were as many as twenty people invited to dine with our family. Her fine china and silverware were always brought out at Thanksgiving. She had a dishwasher she did not use, and she would not let anyone else use either. So, family became the automatic dishwashers. No fun.

One year, my sister Eloise broke a crystal glass. We stared at each other in horror. We quickly gathered up the pieces, wrapped them in a napkin, and put the shattered glass into her purse. She would get rid of the evidence in Manhattan where she lived. We were not prepared to spend a lifetime hearing from my aunt about how we broke one of her expensive crystal pieces.

Aunt Maria loved to entertain, and I enjoyed it when her Cuban friends came to dinner. The Cubans were not pleased when they realized I did not speak Spanish. Because my family was Cuban, they strongly believed that my sister Isabel and I should speak the language. Since we grew up in Canada, my father did not see the need to speak to us in his language. I think my mother played a role in this decision. Later in life my dad regretted his choice.

My aunt was not always happy about the men I brought home. Her looks spoke volumes. She would never offer her opinion—she did not have to. But when I became engaged and subsequently broke off the engagement because I discovered my fiancé already had a wife, she was there for the emotional support I needed.

I will always be grateful to my Cuban American family. They were always there for me. They believed in hard work, education, faith, and being good citizens. I never heard them complain about racism or discrimination. My family was very proud, and if they did experience discrimination they did not share their feelings or experiences with me.

Aunt Maria was a follower of Malcolm X. In fact, when my family visited New York from Nova Scotia one year when I was in my early teens, she took my sister and me to hear and meet this civil rights icon. I guess I was too young at the time to appreciate the significance of that evening, because all I remember about that night is his smile when he said hello to my sister and me.

When I completed my paralegal program, I was certain I would quickly find a job. I was wrong. It took me close to a year before I got my break. Every Sunday, I would search the want ads of the

New York Times. I sent out resumés to no avail. There were many rejection letters, from the places that decided to respond. There were many unsuccessful interviews, and I was becoming discouraged.

Finally I was called for an interview with a Wall Street law firm. When I went for my interview, I felt I had a good chance of being hired. I was first interviewed by the office manager. She called me back for a second interview, this time with the partner I would be working for as a corporate paralegal. The interview went well. Or so I thought. I was very excited because I knew I would be offered the job. Imagine my surprise when I was not hired. I was devastated. I relied on my faith and my family to get me through another rejection.

During this long period of not being able to find paralegal opportunities, I prayed and kept thinking positive thoughts. *Someone is going to hire me as a paralegal.* I had to believe in myself and know that God had a plan for me, in His time and not according to my time. It was almost a year after my interview on Wall Street that I received another call from the office manager. She invited me back to meet with both her and the partner. Apparently, the woman they hired had quit. After the interview I went home and waited for the call. This time I was offered the job. The girl from Whitney Pier was going to work as a corporate paralegal on Wall Street. My family and friends were so excited. I knew this was my opportunity and I was going to ride the train of success. I gave my thanks to God.

My time working on Wall Street was both exciting and fascinating. This was the place that turned me into a workaholic. There were not too many African Americans working there. I was the only Black paralegal and there were no Black attorneys. The few Black people working were either secretaries or file or mailroom clerks. My office was on the first floor, not far from the mailroom. One of the Black secretaries worked on the third floor, and the other on the lower level near the file room where the other Black employee worked. Apparently, they had seen me come for the interviews.

They were not surprised when I did not get the job. Their hopes were raised when they saw me return for another interview months later.

We all became very good friends. With the exception of one, they were all West Indians. In fact, the guys who worked in the mailroom were studying for their university degrees in the evening. I was surprised to learn that one of them was a client. He was a very smart and humble businessman who had many real estate holdings. The Black employee who was one of the workers in the file room was studying at night as well. She was a wiz at science. When she left the firm, she completed her engineering degree. It did not take her long to begin a successful career in her chosen field.

The lawyer I was hired to work for had the reputation of being difficult. It was rumoured that was the reason the other paralegal had left. One of the female lawyers who worked for him took me under her wing and taught me everything I needed to know and more. She was great. Unfortunately for me, she was moving on to work as legal counsel for a bank.

The secretary was a fountain of knowledge. She also made certain that I knew all the administrative details and gave me tips on how to survive in the hectic environment. The guys in the mailroom and my other friends were extremely helpful with what I call "intelligence news." They had my back and I had theirs.

The office manager who reached out to me was also in my corner. Apparently she felt I should have been offered the job over the other candidate. In any event, here I was with great support. I knew I could not and would not fail.

The partner, whom we shall call Bob, was brilliant and a taskmaster. I learned a lot from him and yes, he learned from me. Once he realized I was smart, understood the work, did not watch the clock, and could work under pressure, he began to relax. I don't think he originally believed I would work out. We had many long conversations and finally he admitted he had been afraid to hire

Mayann Francis received a Luminary Award from the University of the West Indies in 2010. (COURTESY OF AUTHOR)

me. He did not think I would fit in. I will always admire him for speaking the truth. If it wasn't for the office manager, who stood her ground and reached out to me a second time, he would have missed the opportunity to learn a valuable lesson about prejudging people because of their skin colour. He also learned never to ask me to make coffee again. The first and only time he asked me to was during a busy closing and because I was the only woman present. I did not protest. When he tasted the coffee, he called his secretary to make another pot. Not sure why. Oh well. I guess it did not taste good. I thought by adding cold water after it was made it would give the coffee a boost and improve the taste. By the look on Bob's face I guess I was wrong.

Even though I failed to make a decent pot of coffee, he became my biggest champion. In fact he joined my aunt in trying to convince me to become a lawyer. When I decided to leave the firm after several years to join a firm in midtown Manhattan, he tried several times to convince me to stay. In the end, he gave me his blessing. He understood the move was a great opportunity.

Incidentally, I was offered the job as a human rights officer with New York City about the same time I got my opportunity on Wall Street. I selected Wall Street because I believed I would have more opportunity to advance my career.

I enjoyed my time on Wall Street. The attorneys I interacted with, both on Wall Street and in the midtown law firm, taught me as much as I wanted to know. I learned the ins and outs of business deals that involved sale and leaseback of equipment. I learned to work with banks and process complex documents. I had to pay attention to detail, be organized, and meet deadlines. Thanks to my mother's sewing club, I was prepared for this aspect of work. My time with the corporate law firms was a great start to my long and blessed career. Working as a paralegal taught me so much about who I am. I had no idea that I could keep up the hectic pace and pressure to stay on top of my files. I enjoyed the work even though it was at times stressful.

My social life was also exciting. New York is indeed "the city that never sleeps." When I was not working, my friends and I would go to Broadway and off-Broadway plays, museums, concerts, restaurants, and attend parties—we knew how to have fun in the Big Apple. I even tried my hand at modelling. Just once. I shook hands with Jesse Jackson and met Star Jones, who was one of the prosecutors at the Brooklyn district attorney's office before she got her big break in Hollywood and on *The View*.

I even had a brief encounter with Harry Belafonte. I used to have my hair attended at a salon on West 72nd Street. One afternoon, I was relaxing in the beautician's chair while she was putting in a blonde weave. Yep, it was blonde! Sometimes it was red! Because the process took hours, I kicked off my shoes, elevated my feet onto a stool, and buried my nose in a book. Someone flicked my toe and said, "You look relaxed." I looked up and said, "Yes, I am." It was Harry Belafonte.

Little did I know that decades later I would be recognized with the Luminary Award from the University of the West Indies at a ceremony in Toronto at the same time Mr. Belafonte would receive the same award. Unfortunately a snowstorm prevented him from accepting his award in person. I was disappointed he was not able to be there. I wanted to remind him how we first met, though I am certain he would not have remembered.

Incidentally, Harry Belafonte visited Halifax in 1978 while I was still living in New York, for a performance at the Rebecca Cohn Auditorium. During his visit, Rocky Jones invited him to his home. This is how Rocky describes the visit in *Revolutionary*:

> *I went backstage and invited him to come and meet some of the young Black kids in Halifax. So he came over to our house. Joan cooked up a chicken curry and fed everybody, as per usual. He stayed for at least three hours. When you look back at it, to be in Nova Scotia and to have an international star like Belafonte just come to your house and sit around, eat chicken curry, and talk to everybody and explain things, it was absolutely amazing. He was good for us, because he was able to explain things that we didn't really know about because he was so very aware.*

Wow, that must have been an exciting evening. One of the youth who was present for Belafonte's visit was George Elliott Clarke, who has written the foreword to this book.

Moving to midtown for work began another interesting chapter in my life. It was not unusual for me to work through the night. Once again I was the only Black person on the legal staff. This time I worked with several partners and the work was more intense. I was glad to have my own office. There were many paralegals who worked in various areas of the corporate firm. A senior paralegal was responsible for our work assignments. As a group we were close and we worked very hard. This firm was much larger than the firm I worked for on Wall Street. My first time driving in a limo was when the firm hired limos to pick up some of their employees during a transit strike. What a thrill! I was the girl from Whitney Pier arriving at work in a limo! I guess this was a taste of what was to come.

My experience on Wall Street was a great foundation for the work that I would become involved with. I loved the work and the people. I made friends with the guys who worked in the mailroom and typing pool. These were critical areas because they were the people you had to rely on if you needed copies made in a hurry or a document typed. Paralegals did not have their own secretaries. We relied on the people in the typing pool. I certainly was not going to alienate them. In the long run, it boils down to treating people with respect and appreciating the work they do.

I have always talked about the value of growing up in Whitney Pier. The diversity of people I was exposed to for over eighteen years gave me the foundation to be open to people with different backgrounds and orientations. Some of the guys who worked in the mailroom and typing pool were gay men who became my friends and protectors, especially at the firm's Christmas parties. The firm knew how to throw a lively, interesting Christmas party for staff. My gay male protectors made sure they stayed close to me. You can use your imagination as to why. Just as I learned a lot in the office, I observed and learned a lot more at the parties.

One of my protectors frequently attended Studio 54. I also attended Studio 54, for private functions. This famous nightclub opened in 1977, and people would stand in line for hours hoping to gain entry. Someone would peruse the line and give you the nod to go into the club. My friend, whom we shall call Jack, wanted me to go with him one evening. I did not go because I thought I would not get in and I did not feel like standing in the long lines that always formed. When I explained this the next day, Jack was not pleased. Hands on his hips, he gave me a strange look. "My dear, you would have gotten the nod without any problem." I guess I will never know whether or not he was right.

There was a young man, a high school student, who worked in the mailroom during the summer months. For whatever reason, this young fellow decided that I would be his friend. He was a very nice kid who loved to talk and pull tricks. I used to ask my fellow paralegals, "Why me?" As paralegals we were very busy and there was no time for visits or casual conversation. Telling him this was like talking to a wall. Maybe he thought of me as the big sister he never had. He was relentless. As time flew by, I watched him grow from an annoying boy into an intelligent, caring young man. Even though he teased me frequently, I was very fond of him. He was a very nice person with a kind heart. He went on to become a doctor. Currently he is director of the Center for Transformative Geriatric Research at Johns Hopkins Hospital in Baltimore, and is married and a proud dad. We are still in contact.

There were many long days and nights. One summer, my mother was visiting from Sydney. Unfortunately it was one of the busiest times for the type of files assigned to me. We had many deals to prepare for and close. This always meant long days and nights. When I arrived home in the early morning, my mother could not understand. I don't think she believed I was at work. She became even more incensed when I informed her that I was only home long enough to freshen up and then I was going back to the office. She relaxed a bit when I told her my transportation was provided. I think she was worried about my taking public transportation.

I must say, I enjoyed the hectic pace. Not all of my cohorts were able to take the pressure of working long hours and juggling numerous files for several senior corporate partners. One day one of the paralegals could not handle it. Her office was next door to mine. I offered to do some of her work but she was determined to quit. And she did. I was sad to see her go because we had become great friends. I was a bridesmaid at her wedding. She married a wonderful man who happened to be a lawyer. We caught up with one another about five years ago. She lives in Arizona with her husband.

As time passed, I knew that I wanted to attend graduate school. My sister Eloise was studying for her master's in nutrition at New York University (NYU). I knew this was the university I wanted to attend. She was a great role model. She demonstrated so much discipline as a married, mature student, studying and working full-time. We were very proud of her when she graduated.

I attended NYU at night for my master's in public administration because I was still working at the law firm. The law firm was fine with this as long as I made myself available when needed. Sometimes I had to return to the firm to complete work that had to be ready for the next morning. Some nights, I was very tired. I would often stay with Eloise in Manhattan and not travel back to Brooklyn alone on the subway late at night. Still, I had to own up to my responsibilities. That's the way it was. When I wanted to give up, I did not. I thought about Eloise and how hard she worked to complete her graduate degree.

Graduate school was a happy time. In my final semester, I decided to attend university full-time. The firm was so accommodating. They told me to call them if I needed to work and they would find a spot for me. I guess my hard work paid off. Fortunately I was fine. I was very proud to be nominated for a presidential internship program in Washington while I was in graduate school at NYU. Even though I did not get the posting, I was thrilled to have been nominated.

After graduation it did not take long to secure a position as a personnel representative with the New York City Law Department, also known as the Office of the Corporation Counsel. Among other things, the law department represents the city, the mayor, other elected officials, and the City's many agencies in civil litigation.

I left the Office of the Corporation Counsel in 1986 and joined the Brooklyn District Attorney's Office in their personnel department. Elizabeth Holtzman, famous for the Watergate investigation, was the district attorney. Prior to her election as district attorney, she was a congresswoman and a member of the House Judiciary Committee that voted for the impeachment of President Richard Nixon. Joe Hines succeeded Ms. Holtzman as the Brooklyn district attorney. Under his tenure, the office was famous for the prosecution of the Howard Beach and Bensonhurst cases.

In the former, twenty-three-year-old Michael Griffith, an African American, died in 1986 after being accidentally hit by a car when he tried to escape from a group of white youths in Howard Beach, Queens. The prosecution and trial led to convictions and prison terms for the gang members for causing the death of Mr. Griffith.

In the Bensonhurst case, sixteen-year-old Yusef Hawkins was murdered in 1989. A gang of about thirty white teens—armed with a gun and baseball bats—shot and killed him because they thought he was dating a white woman in their Brooklyn neighbourhood. Joseph Fama, age nineteen, was convicted of second-degree murder. He was sentenced to thirty-two and one-third years to life in prison. In 2022 he will be eligible for parole. Separate trials for the other attackers also resulted in convictions.

Working for the District Attorney's Office opened my eyes to many types of crimes, like child abuse, sexual assault, murder, and drug trafficking, all of which made their way through the system. There was no doubt that the lawyers and undercover cops, executives, support staff, and administrative staff were extremely busy. The office was humming twenty-four hours a day.

There are two incidents I remember very vividly. Late one afternoon, shortly after I joined the personnel department, the director asked if I would be working late. I told him yes. He suggested that I take a break and go home early. Of course my personality led me to ignore him. Five minutes went by and he realized I was still at my desk. He insisted that I leave. He stood there until I packed my things and left. I was puzzled by his behaviour and was annoyed because I wanted to finish a project. Everyone was gone except for some people in the adjacent offices.

When I went into work the next morning he told me why he wanted me to leave the office. Next door to our department, a sting operation was carried out, resulting in the arrest of several workers throughout the District Attorney's Office. A few weeks prior to this, there was a new hire, who turned out to be an undercover cop. The police had previously bugged the office where the sting took place. One of the workers in the office was arrested for trafficking drugs. She was led out in handcuffs that evening. Others were arrested the next day. Some people either lost their job or were suspended.

The second incident was so horrific that just thinking about it makes me sad. One of the women who worked in the narcotics department suffered the loss of her daughter. The daughter's husband viciously murdered her. Because the murder took place in Brooklyn, the crime fell under the jurisdiction of the Brooklyn DA's office. It was a very sad time for everyone.

By the time I left the DA's office in 1990, I had earned the title of administrative manager. Once again my hard work, commitment, and belief in continuous learning paid off. My determination to succeed and survive in the Big Apple is a testament to the early childhood lessons taught to me by my parents and the community of Whitney Pier. There were times that I wanted to give up and return home to Nova Scotia. Deep in my heart, I knew that if I kept trying, everything would be all right. I had support from my American friends, mentors on many of the jobs I held, and of course my family. I even contemplated entering city politics.

I will always cherish my time living and working in the United States, despite the rather sensational events. I have no regrets about having stayed sixteen years. I made many friends there. And it was an opportunity to spend time with my Cuban American family. That period in my life was exciting, sad, educational, and a period of self-growth. I learned a great deal about myself. I not only experienced the pain of love, but I also learned the joy of love. My love was a mature, handsome, fun, intelligent, respectful young man. I have beautiful and treasured memories about the time we spent together, even though it was less than a year. We had so much fun and respect for each other. It was beautiful.

When I arrived in New York, I was separated from my husband and fearful of the future. I had no job. And I was living with the knowledge that I might soon lose my eyesight. When I left New York, my peripheral vision was narrower but I still had a strong central vision. Somehow I found the courage to charge forward, even though I had not yet developed strategies to manage my disability. My faith played a key role in how I would approach the future.

When I said goodbye to New York to return to Halifax, I was a changed person—confident about who I was as a Black woman. Having been surrounded by so many role models made me feel proud. I am grateful to the mentors who took me under their wings and guided me along my American journey. One of the many lessons I learned was not to discriminate about whom you can learn from. Life is about learning and giving. My mentors were men, women, gay, Hispanic, Black, white, Jewish, Democrat, Republican, professional, and non-professional, grassroots people—people from different walks of life. Collectively, along with my family, everyone helped shape who I am today. I owe all of them a debt of gratitude.

At my farewell party at the District Attorney's Office, DA Joe Hines joked about not knowing I was a Canadian—he thought I was one of them. Actually, I was one of them. Both Isabel and I have dual citizenship. My parents registered us at birth as children born abroad of American parents (they were naturalized Americans). One of the senior lawyers told me he sensed that my wings were going to spread when I returned to Canada. He was right, wasn't he.

Chapter 5

FROM NEW YORK TO HALIFAX TO TORONTO

The Lord will protect you from all danger; he will keep you safe. He will protect you as you come and go now and forever.

PSALM 121:7–8

L eaving New York after living there for sixteen years was difficult. I would be leaving my friends and family. I had fallen in love with the Big Apple. Even though I was returning home to Nova Scotia, I was nervous—I wondered how I would fit in after being away for more than a decade.

Isabel had called me in early 1990. She said a family friend wanted to speak to me about a job opportunity in Halifax. This person had told my sister that she believed I would be a perfect match for a position at Dalhousie University, a well-known, prestigious university, both nationally and internationally. I initially told my sister that I was not interested in returning to Halifax because I was very happy in New York. Besides, I was preparing to make application for a second master's degree at the New School for Social Research, in New York City. She asked me to think about it before I made a final decision.

A few weeks went by before the woman called my sister again. I gave my sister permission to give her my number. When the family friend called, we talked in great detail about the position; she eventually arranged for me to speak with the head of human resources at the university. After a telephone interview with Mr. Mike Roughneen, I was invited to Halifax to be interviewed by key members from the university community.

After these intense interviews, I returned to New York. Why did I change my mind about moving back to Halifax? Apart from my interest in the position, my mother was getting older. In Halifax, I would be nearer to Sydney where my mother lived with Isabel, who was her main caregiver. Isabel had returned to Sydney in 1982 shortly after our father's death, when her husband became pastor of our church. Being in Halifax would give me more of an opportunity to share in our mother's care. It was only after I was offered and accepted the position of employment equity officer that reality set in about leaving the city I had grown to love.

When I told my friends I was returning to Canada, they were sad but felt I was making the right decision. The DA's office gave me a leave of absence for six months, just in case I wanted to return. I was deeply moved by their offer. The ensuing months were filled with farewell dinners and parties. There were tears and promises to visit Nova Scotia. My desire to earn a second master's and a doctorate were put on hold. I left New York with a heavy heart. I guess somehow I knew that I would never again live in the city I loved. I would visit often, but I would no longer be a New Yorker.

I began my employment as Dalhousie's first employment equity officer on August 6, 1990. I was the first senior administrator hired to assist faculties and administrative units plan and implement programs of employment equity for women, visible minorities, Aboriginals, and persons with disabilities. My position was a direct report to the president of the university. The reporting relationship is very important when implementing change. This relationship sent a strong signal that the university was serious about employment equity. *Employment equity* was a term that I was not familiar with. In the United States the comparable term was *affirmative action*. The term *employment equity* was coined by the Honourable Rosalie Abella, now Justice of the Supreme Court of Canada.

At the same time that the Employment Equity Act was proclaimed law, Canada Immigration and Employment established the federal contractors program. Dalhousie fell under this umbrella and had to comply with the requirements, which included a census of the Dalhousie workforce and establishment of goals and timetables.

There was plenty of work to be done under employment equity. Still there are people who believe employment equity was not necessary because inequality in hiring did not exist—qualified people were hired to fill positions, and that's all that mattered. A common misconception was that employment equity, or affirmative action, meant hiring people only to satisfy a quota system, but of course, that's not the case.

Change would be difficult. People fear change. Change for some people represents a loss. Whether in a university or elsewhere, there are those who see change as a challenge to their comfort level—they desire to just keep things the way they are. They refuse to recognize and understand that change is necessary if the organization is to grow, flourish, and be competitive.

I was aware of these challenges, so when I assumed the role of employment equity officer, I thought it was important to knock on doors, for people to meet me. I wanted them to ask those difficult questions about employment equity and how it would affect them if they were not members of one of the target groups. I wanted to make certain any incorrect information or myths about equity—or about me—were dispelled. I also made countless presentations throughout the campus. Communication with individuals and groups about the change the university was set to undergo was extremely important for the success of the implementation. It was critical to hold awareness sessions about discrimination and stereotypical assumptions. It simply was not sufficient to recruit more members of the target groups; it was important to create a welcoming and non-hostile environment. In other words, it was important to ensure that the university, through training and honest, open dialogue, created an atmosphere where equity groups felt safe and respected and all employees felt comfortable. Dalhousie University also had a sexual harassment office that was very important and busy, and my office worked with it very closely.

Working toward implementation of employment equity was a challenging but rewarding undertaking. I was honoured to play a role in leading the university through a process of change that would create a more inclusive and welcoming environment.

I want to stress that all organizations, whether a private corporation, government, or university, must put in place effective mechanisms to monitor the progress of their policies on a regular basis. Commitment and accountability to employment equity and inclusivity must come from the top. And above all, there must be clear, measurable, meaningful results. Among the many other areas on which managers are evaluated, they must also be evaluated on their performance as it relates to employment equity, diversity, and harassment. How welcoming is the organization's environment? Is there a problem with retention of target groups? If so, why? What feedback is the organization receiving regarding target group hires? These are critical questions every organization must ask if inclusivity is to succeed.

Life at Dalhousie kept me very busy. I was not too busy, however, to notice the environment beyond the walls of the university. In some ways my return to Halifax was disappointing. I was glad to be home near my family and close friends. And I liked my role at the university. I was not, however, prepared for what I did not see. It seemed that I returned to a city and province where time stood still.

In 1991 I went into a store on Barrington Street and found myself completely ignored by the proprietor. The proprietor's attention was devoted to the white customers. After waiting for some time I left the store in frustration. This incident prompted me to write an article for the *Dalhousie News*, titled "Facing Racism: Little has changed in Halifax."

> *What I have experienced since my return home goes to the core of my dignity and my pride as a human being. I certainly did not expect a bed of roses. Neither did I expect a bed of racism. Thank heavens for those people of good will in the dominant group who want change and demonstrate a global vision and understanding of other racial groups. Am I glad to be back home in my birthplace? I am happy to be home near my family and very close friends. I am comfortable with myself as a woman of colour, but I am uncomfortable in a city and province that is uncomfortable with me because my skin, the skin of my race, is black. How very sad. It is even sadder when my Black friends say, "That's the way it is. You'll get used to it."*

I began to wonder if I had made a mistake returning to Nova Scotia. I had left vibrant, diverse New York City to return home only to discover that diversity was virtually non-existent. And people seemed to bury their heads in the sand about systemic and overt racism.

I am not certain what I was thinking, but I was expecting among other things to go into stores and not be followed or ignored.

I also expected more salespeople who looked like me. I was very optimistic about returning to Halifax, because I thought the mayor was Black. When I think about this now, I have to laugh at my ignorance. I had a poor photocopy of a newspaper clipping of then mayor Ron Wallace. The photo was dark and I incorrectly assumed he was Black. After all, I lived in New York on November 7, 1989, when David Dinkins was the first Black person to be elected mayor of New York City. He served as mayor from 1990 to 1993. Anyway, I didn't discover my error until I mentioned to a friend that things were looking up in Halifax because the mayor was Black. They thought I was joking. They very quickly gave me a dose of reality, telling me that little had changed in the sixteen years I'd been away. Needless to say, I was disappointed and sad to hear this. Halifax has not yet had a mayor from any racial minority. In 1973, Graham Downey became the first Black city councillor; he served until 2000. In 2016 Lindell Smith became only the second Black person to be elected to Halifax City Council.

I was surprised to learn that my article attracted a wide audience. It made the local news. I was invited to talk about racism and my observations on CBC Radio. People reached out to me from other parts of Canada; they were surprised and disappointed by what they read. People asked how they could help to bring about change. The outreach from people was very encouraging.

I think the article received attention for a couple of reasons. People had been burying their heads in the sand for a very long time. "I am not racist," some would say, "I have Black friends and I attend Black events." Really! The notion of systemic racism or unconscious bias was not something people understood or wanted to understand. Everyone holds unconscious beliefs about other social identity groups, which stem from one's tendency to organize social worlds by categorizing. Unconscious bias is far more prevalent than conscious prejudice and is often even incompatible with one's conscious values.

Because I was born and raised in Nova Scotia, attended a prestigious graduate school in the United States, had a solid work record in New York City, and was now employed by a well-known and highly respected university, my article had credibility. Had I not left the province and written the same article, would people have noticed?

Many people were embarrassed and shocked, especially when I pointed out that I left the province sixteen years earlier when there were no Black people working in retail on Barrington Street. Time had stood still; as far as I could see the current situation was the same. I challenged people to walk through shopping centres and count the number of Black people working in the stores. I also pointed out the absence of Black people in media, government, school boards, universities, and private industry. People had a difficult time refuting what I had said. Some people believed the Black population was not very large and that was why we were not visible. People continue, even today, to deny that racism is alive and well.

The manager of the building where I was living at the time mentioned that one of the tenants was surprised to see me because she thought Black people were not allowed in the building. She was not objecting to my being there; she was simply surprised and pleased to see that I was living there. Wow!

Because of the article and my position at Dalhousie University, I received many speaking engagements. I used these opportunities to educate the audience on the realities of inequalities in society. It was never my intent to make people feel guilty or become angry. I wanted people to open their minds to what they were hearing. I asked the audience to resist becoming defensive. I would ask them to relax and understand that they needed to know what they did not know.

In 1993, I spoke to the Multicultural Health Association about racism and discrimination. In part, this is what I said.

Because racism and discrimination come from within, we must each fulfil our obligation to change. We must stop and think about our personal response to the multicultural face of Canadian society. To do this requires a degree of honesty and courage that we may not have displayed in the past. Recognizing that the process of socialization has incorporated racism and discrimination into our psyche, we must face it head on. After all, the true evil is not having practised racism and discrimination in the past but failing to do something about that behaviour in the present and future. Racism, I continue to say, is like a disease. It can be active or it can lie dormant, waiting to infect all it touches. When it attacks, its victims are demoralized and dehumanized. If the attacks continue and there is no medicine to control or stop their spread, the self-esteem of its victims slowly dies. The pain continues to eat at the core of one's dignity and self-respect. While racism affects all of us, it affects each person differently. A white child who, through socialization, is brought up to believe that their race is the norm by which all other cultures are judged exotic, colourful, or primitive, is left out of touch with the rest of the world. These kinds of assumptions are the foundation upon which overt and systemic racism are built. Conversely, a non-white child may find their development already proscribed by the racial expectations of the dominant group. It is soon discovered that being non-white entails a constant daily battle. When the child becomes an adult, they may believe that they are inferior and subsequently their potential to develop as a person is arrested. Or they may grow up angry and resentful.

Even though I wrote those words almost thirty years ago, unfortunately they ring true today. It was not easy growing up Black. I am proud to be Black, but it takes work not to have your spirit broken by the barriers and the attitudes that confront you. I kept my spirit, never allowing it to be broken. For me it is about courage and love of self and confidence in my abilities. Every day I wake up knowing that there is a possibility I will face racism and discrimination. It may not be overt. It could be as simple as being made to feel invisible, or that your opinion does not matter. Instead, someone will make the decision for you, even without asking you. This is reality. Nonetheless, through it all, I stay strong, happy, and steadfast. My spirit may bend, but I will not allow it to be broken.

Living in New York helped because I saw successful people who looked like me. Role models are very important for the Black child. In fact, I think it is important that all children see people of different racial or cultural backgrounds working as teachers, bankers, journalists, professors, engineers, store clerks, and so on. Failure to see people of various races and cultures in a variety of roles sends the signal that only a particular group of people are qualified and capable of performing in our society.

We must never underestimate the effect that the institution of slavery had on society. The slave owners succeeded in convincing the world that Black people were inferior, not trustworthy, lazy. These myths have been passed down from generation to generation, resulting in economic and educational disadvantages for Black people—discrimination and racism prevented them from full participation in society. I am mindful of those slaves who fought and died for freedom. It is the legacy of strength, courage, and hope for a better future that I choose to embrace to counter the dark, evil legacy of slavery.

I was excited when in 1992 I was appointed to serve on the Canadian Advisory Council on the Status of Women for a period of three years. The council was established in 1973 in response to the Royal Commission on the Status of Women in Canada. The council's mandate at the time was not only to advise the federal government but also to keep the public informed about issues affecting women. The head of the council was Dr. Glenda Simms, a Black woman, appointed in 1989 by Prime Minister Brian Mulroney.

Glenda was a very powerful leader and committed advocate for women who was in demand as a speaker both nationally and internationally. In 1994 when the University of Manitoba conferred on her an honorary doctorate, it described her as having a long-standing commitment to Aboriginal peoples, women, racial minorities, community issues, and public service. Dr. Simms eventually returned to her native Jamaica.

I was happy about this appointment because I wanted to make a difference in women's lives, especially women who did not have a voice. I believed my position at the university would also assist me in identifying issues to take to the national table. I travelled to many parts of Nova Scotia making presentations related to the council's work and listening to women's concerns about physical violence, sexual harassment, racism and discrimination, sexual assault, and many other issues. I hope that our work had an impact on women and other members of the public about their rights and the organizations available to help them.

Another great opportunity was when I was appointed to the Nova Scotia Barristers Council, as a lay member. I also served on the Metro United Way and the Indigenous Blacks and Mi'kmaq Law Program at Dalhousie, now renamed the Indigenous Blacks and Mi'kmaq Initiative. Serving on these boards was truly a blessing. Each board gave me an opportunity to make a difference not only in race relations but also in many other areas that affect people's lives.

Even though these appointments added to my hectic schedule, I thought it was important that I contribute to positive change. I wanted to try to make people open their eyes to the injustices around us, in particular for Black Nova Scotians and for all women. I wanted to see a dialogue on race and gender not only on the university campus, but also in the wider society. If we fail to speak honestly about our fears and concerns, we only continue to perpetuate myths and stereotypes.

Because my return to Halifax had been recent, I was surprised when the Black community selected me to serve on a committee to investigate an incident that took place in the city. In the early morning hours of July 19, 1991, there was a disturbance in downtown Halifax between Blacks and whites, which eventually led to allegations of police using excessive force against Black men. Two Black men were denied access to a bar on Argyle Street, and this apparently triggered the incident. It may have been a matter of "the straw that broke the camel's back," as there were rumours that other Black people had also been denied entry to clubs on different occasions. Some people referred to that dreadful night as the Halifax Race Riot. Once again the spotlight was on race relations in Nova Scotia, not only locally but nationally as well.

In 1989 there had been a fight between Black and white youths at Cole Harbour High School in Dartmouth, the city across the harbour from Halifax. Officials had to close the school because of the seriousness of the incident. The fight resulted in a variety of charges. Students and parents said tensions had existed between Black and white students for years prior to the fight. And of course, there was the injustice that happened to the Black community of Africville in 1969 when the city destroyed it in the name of industrial development.

After the evening of July 19, 1991, there were numerous meetings among Black citizens—called Black family meetings—and between Black citizens and police, government officials, and concerned white groups. No one wanted to see a repeat of the evening in July. People wanted solutions. The chief of police, Vincent MacDonald, set up a committee to look into the allegations of police brutality on that ill-fated night. Besides myself, the appointed civilian members were Reverend Donald Skeir, pastor of churches in North and East Preston, Cherry Brook, and Lake Loon, and Reverend Calvin Symonds, pastor of Cornwallis Street Baptist Church (now called New Horizons Baptist Church) in Halifax. The

Halifax Police Department was represented by Inspector Dave Murphy, former Chief of Police Frank Beazley, and Constable Mark Hobeck.

We were expected to produce one report, but because of disagreement about the final contents, in December 1991 we instead issued two reports, one of them prepared by the civilian members. The civilian report was critical of police action on the night of July 19. Needless to say, because two reports were produced, one highly critical of police actions, it attracted the attention of many news outlets. It was our hope that the second report would generate discussion and bring the community and the police department together in an honest and open dialogue. For us it was about building a community based on trust and greater understanding between police and community members so that future generations of young Black boys and girls might one day aspire to be police officers.

Being one of the members of the review committee was a rewarding experience. I learned things about police officers and police work that I hadn't fully grasped beforehand. My hope was that our report would be a catalyst for change.

My work at Dalhousie and my community involvement gave me many opportunities to deliver speeches and workshops and attend meetings in Halifax, Ottawa, and other parts of Canada, where I was able to deliver messages about inequity and have discussions with audiences about social justice.

Now when I speak to audiences, especially youth and young adults, I tell them that you never know who is watching your performance both inside and outside the organization, regardless of where you are employed or the committees you belong to. One of the blessings in my life is that after Wall Street, every opportunity that presented itself to me was because someone called and suggested I submit my name for an excellent career opportunity.

While working at Dalhousie, I received a call from someone in Ontario, suggesting that I submit my name for the position of assistant deputy minister of the Ontario Women's Directorate (OWD). Incidentally, a close friend in Halifax had seen the position advertised in the *Globe and Mail* and suggested I should apply. To my friend, I flatly said, "No way." A few weeks later, I got a call from the deputy minister responsible for recruitment for this position. He said he'd heard positive reports about me and wondered if I had applied. When I said no, he suggested I think about applying. I ended up leaving Dalhousie in late 1993 to move to Ontario. When I left the university, I believed it was ready to move forward with equity.

I would be the first African Canadian to hold the position of assistant deputy minister for the OWD. Little did I know that this role would be one of the most challenging of my career. There was resistance, even though the Black women who worked there embraced me, and my executive assistant, who was white, was a great supporter—and fellow cat lover. We still keep in touch.

I joined the organization at a time when change was needed. I knew trying to bring about change in the current environment of resistance would be difficult. It would also be a major challenge because I found the place hostile. Life at the OWD was not easy. By the time I left the organization, I was not certain if I wanted to lead an all-women's organization going forward. My experience at the OWD left a sour taste in my mouth. With the passage of time I finally got past it.

I believe some of the women—not the Black women who "had my back"—were glad to see me go. Nonetheless, as unhappy as I was at the OWD, I was glad I had the experience. As I said earlier, every opportunity prepares you for the next, and each job has something to teach you.

When speaking to young people, I tell them not to discount jobs they did while in college or high school. For example, working at McDonald's or Tim Hortons, you learn customer service, teamwork, responsibility, and accountability. These are transferrable people skills. Someone asked, "What about a job delivering newspapers?"

Once again, you learn responsibility: someone is waiting for you to deliver the morning paper. A woman told me that she does not get out much but enjoys her cup of coffee and sitting down to read two newspapers every morning. She said she would be lost without her papers. So you see, without even being aware of it, by delivering the newspaper and taking your responsibility seriously, you are bringing joy to someone.

A positive outcome of working at the OWD was being selected by the Institute of Public Administration of Canada to represent Ontario at a women's conference in Accra, Ghana. At the conference, in July 1996, I presented a paper titled "The Impact of Economic Reforms on the Condition of Women in Africa." Attending this conference with women from all over West Africa was the highlight of my life to that point. I had never been at a conference where all of the women had PhDs, spoke several languages, and were Black. I was embraced with affection and respect. I was the sister who had left the continent generations ago. They prayed over me and told me to take their prayers and love home with me. I was struck by their wealth of knowledge and their warmth. They even taught me a few African dance steps.

During a break in our schedules, I went on a tour to Elmina Castle, built by the Portuguese in 1482, where slaves were kept and treated worse than animals. The governor preyed on the female slaves. Whenever he felt like it, he would look into the pit and point to the woman he wanted to have sex with. If she refused, she was beaten and left with open wounds in the pit, under the hot sun.

In the dungeon, I could feel the arms of the slaves reaching out to me, crying for help. I cried, overwhelmed with emotion. Standing in this small cave, I was trying to imagine what my ancestors had gone through. I felt their bodies, all over me, pulling me and crying along with me. I wanted to scream because I was helpless. When I felt their grip loosen and they let me go, I knew my life and my outlook would never be the same. My ancestors' spirits permeated my soul. I was sad but at the same time I was empowered and stronger as a Black woman. They gave me the courage to spread my wings and soar. Their spirits would always hold me up; I would be standing on their shoulders. I left Africa with a sense of sisterhood. My African sisters sent me back to Canada with a renewed sense of purpose and who I was—a proud Black woman.

The minister responsible for the Ontario Women's Directorate from 1991 to 1995 was Marion Boyd. She was also the justice minister, an extremely intelligent woman whose staff were very efficient. Her executive assistant was Angela Robertson, a Black woman whom I referred to as the Queen of Strategy and someone I admired, and still do, for her intelligence and her fight for social justice. In 2017 she was awarded an honorary Doctor of Laws degree from York University. She is an amazing woman. Minister Boyd was a great listener. She did not always agree with me, but I knew she respected me, listened, understood the issues, and she was fair. I learned a great deal from her and her staff.

In 1997 legislation was introduced that would change municipal structure, finance, and function in Ontario. As a result of this legislation, the Provincial-Municipal Education and Training Secretariat (PMETS) was mandated "to identify education and training needs relating to the smooth transfer of service responsibility to the municipal sector, to find ways to meet these needs, and to coordinate the activities of provincial and municipal providers of education and training activities." I was transferred from the OWD to PMETS as assistant deputy minister. I was very grateful for this change. The challenge was again a difficult one, but I was so happy to take it on.

The provincial government had moved certain responsibilities from the province to the municipalities, a move that was not without controversy. PMETS had a three-year mandate. I was surrounded with great people who were respectful, kind, and excited about the work we had to do, and we worked well as a team. We believed that during this change process, both the municipal and provincial levels of government should learn from each other. As ADM I did not want our team to assume an attitude that we had all the answers. I believed it was important that learning take place on both sides. All parties must be involved in the change process. This was a critical period for the provincial and municipal governments in Ontario, and it was a privilege to have played a role in the history of Ontario municipal/provincial relations. Months after I relocated to Nova Scotia in 1999, PMETS was recognized for its important work.

I often felt that God opened the door for me to live and work in Toronto for a reason. I had been excited to be in a large and diverse city. While I was in Halifax in the early 1990s, I gave serious thought to moving back to New York. The lack of diversity in Halifax and the racial situation there was taking a toll on me. I believe my time in Toronto prepared me for my eventual return to Halifax, not New York.

Chapter 6

MY TWO ANGELS

Hold fast to dreams
For if dreams die
Life is a broken-winged bird
That cannot fly.

-LANGSTON HUGHES, "DREAMS," FROM THE ANTHOLOGY
GOLDEN SLIPPERS: AN ANTHOLOGY OF NEGRO POETRY FOR
YOUNG READERS, ED. ARNA BONTEMPS (1941)

While I was living in Toronto, my friend, role model, and mentor, Beverly Mascoll, introduced me to very interesting and wonderful people. I met many Black women and men who were activists, politicians, business people, artists, bankers, entrepreneurs, doctors, lawyers, teachers, principals, writers, professors...it was amazing. I felt I was back in New York.

I first met Beverly in Halifax in the early 1990s when the two of us were guest speakers at an event. Beverly, a highly successful entrepreneur, was the keynote speaker. I had heard about her many years earlier. Her husband was from Sydney. Those of us from Whitney Pier teased Emerson (Emmy) Mascoll that he was a wannabe "Pier dear" because apparently he spent a great deal of time there.

Beverly was a successful businesswoman and recipient of the Order of Canada. She received many awards for her success as a businesswoman, her philanthropy, and community leadership. She established the Beverly Mascoll Community Foundation in 2004, of which I was happy to be a member. We gave financial awards to individuals and not-for-profit organizations. She cared about people. Her philanthropy went beyond her own community and her beloved country, Canada. And she had an amazing sense of humour. She once loaned me five dollars because I had left my wallet at home. Anyone who knows me knows that if I borrow twenty-five cents from you, I will pay you back. Anyway, I knew that I would not see Bev for a few weeks, so I decided to mail her a cheque. She called me and asked, "What were you thinking?" After all, we were friends. After she finished lecturing me, I laughed and said, "Bev, you are a businesswoman, did you cash the cheque?" She burst out laughing and said, "Yes, I did." The two of us laughed so hard we could no longer talk.

When I first met Bev, she was everything I had imagined. She was beautiful, kind, friendly, and down-to-earth. From that day, we became close friends. I told her how much I admired her and that I was preparing to order beauty products from her business, because it was not easy to find hair, skin care, and makeup products for Black women in Halifax. Bev did not miss a beat. She took my order and indicated that when she returned to Toronto she would immediately place it. And she did. Within a week of her return to Toronto, I had my beauty products.

We often discussed her success. She told me that Nova Scotia–born Viola Desmond and America's Madam C. J. Walker influenced her direction. Both were successful Black businesswomen in the beauty supply business. Madam Walker was the first Black millionaire in the United States.

Beverly often talked about her early days in the business. Her very close and loyal friend Gloria was with Beverly from the start of Bev's venture into the world of business and remained her loyal friend right up until Bev died. The two of them would make me laugh with stories of their travel to beauty shows in the US and Canada, promoting the business.

Beverly was born in Fall River, Nova Scotia, on October 29, 1941, then moved to Toronto with her family in the 1950s. In 1993, Beverly and her husband were invited to Fall River to unveil a plaque at the elementary school bearing the name of three Black women who played a crucial role in the Fall River community, one of whom, Martha Ash, was Beverly's grandmother. Beverly was very proud to know that Ash Lee Jefferson Elementary School carried the name of her grandmother and two other deserving and highly respected Black women, Ada Lee and Selena Jefferson. All three women were known for their humanitarian work.

When I relocated to Toronto, Beverly was ecstatic. She helped me find a place to live. With a smile, she said, "One's address is important." She and her husband hosted a party in their home where I was the guest of honour. She wanted to make sure that I met people who were leaders, not only in their respective communities, but also in their field of work or in their activism. I was overwhelmed and deeply moved. I credit Beverly for the relative ease with which I adapted to living in Toronto. Both she and her husband were there whenever I needed their help.

Beverly was a very compassionate and caring person. One time when I was home ill, she called to see if I needed anything. I told her I had sufficient food. She didn't say anything other than "Oh." Within one hour, she was at my door with a bag of groceries. All she said was, "I know you need this. See you later." And she left.

I admired Beverly's commitment to excellence. She always remarked, if you are going to do something, regardless what it is, then make certain that you perform at the highest level you

Beverly Mascoll was a friend, role model, and mentor to Mayann Francis. Mascoll graduated in 2000 from York University with a Bachelor of Arts in Women's Studies.
(YORK UNIVERSITY)

are capable of. Beverly was one of the leaders who helped raise funds to establish the first Chair in Black Canadian Studies at Dalhousie University. Beverly and her husband established scholarships for African Canadian students at universities in Ontario and Nova Scotia. Education was very important to her. She invited me to lunch one afternoon saying she had something to tell me and that she wanted my feedback. She told me she had always wanted to attend university. Her husband and son encouraged her to follow her dream. She applied to York University and was accepted. I was so excited for her. Here was a successful businesswoman fulfilling her dream of acquiring a degree that had escaped her when she was younger. Beverly was fifty-five years old. I strongly believe in continuous learning, and here was Bev living what I believe. We are never too old or too successful to continue learning, whether in a formal or informal setting. I told her she had my full support in whatever way she might need me. She continued to manage her business, serve on boards, and be a devoted wife and mother while studying. My admiration for her only increased.

Bev graduated from York University with her Bachelor of Arts in Women's Studies in June 2000. I was honoured to watch her walk across the platform to receive her degree. Fourteen years later, in 2014, I would be awarded an honorary doctorate from Bev's alma mater. Her husband, Emerson, came to celebrate this honour. I included Bev in my address to the graduates. I told them that she was an alumna who was my friend, role model, advisor, and a successful businesswoman. I added that I felt her presence on that special day.

In April 2000, Mayann Francis received the prestigious Harry Jerome Award for professional excellence. She had been nominated by her friend Bev Mascoll. (ADAMS PHOTOGRAPHY)

In 2000, Beverly surprised me by nominating me for a Harry Jerome Award for professional excellence. I was awarded this prestigious honour in April 2000. In my acceptance speech, I thanked Bev for being my friend, mentor, and role model. I referred to her as an angel God had brought into my life. I would never have imagined that by May 2001 she would be dead. Bev knew at the time that she had breast cancer but chose not to tell me because she did not want to ruin my special night. She waited until I returned home to Halifax to break the news to me about her recent diagnosis. She told me not to worry because she planned to fight the cancer. We stayed in touch during her treatment. She was undergoing treatment when she graduated from York.

In 2014, Mayann Francis received an honorary doctorate from York University. She remembered her late friend Bev Mascoll in her address to the graduates. (YORK UNIVERSITY)

Still, I was not prepared for her phone call on May 9, 2001, when she told me she only had two weeks to live. I was shattered. Bev was calm. She was consoling me instead of the other way around. I flew to Toronto and along with a few close friends, including Gloria, sat on the floor surrounding our beloved Bev as she sat in a chair talking to us about health care. She still looked beautiful. The only giveaway that there was a problem was the oxygen tank and her shortness of breath. Bev approached her illness as a businesswoman. She told us to learn about the health system. Know what questions to ask, what we are entitled to, and what to insist on. She also emphasized the importance of breast self-examination and regular mammograms. As I sat there in her bedroom listening to her words of wisdom, I did not want to accept that she was dying.

The bedroom was exceptionally large. At one end was a large fireplace surrounded by stuffed toys and one large ragdoll. For some reason I was fixated with the doll. I had seen the doll before; this time, however, I could not stop looking at it. My fascination with the doll baffled me. It seemed as though I was not in control of my gaze. Weeks after Bev's death, I would come to understand the significance of my preoccupation with the ragdoll.

During a quiet moment with Bev she asked me to read her favourite psalm, Psalm 121.

I look to the mountains;
Where will my help come from?
My help will come from the Lord,
Who made heaven and earth.
He will not let you fall;
Your protector is always awake.
The protector of Israel never dozes or sleeps.
The Lord will guard you: he is by your side to protect you.
The sun will not hurt you during the day. Nor the moon during
   the night.
The Lord will protect you from all danger: he will keep you safe.
He will protect you as you come and go now and for ever.

I put the Bible down and held her hand. She smiled and said, "I dreamt of my grandmother last night. We were in our kitchen in Fall River. She is waiting for me."

Beverly was planning a trip to Nova Scotia to receive an honorary doctorate from Mount Saint Vincent University in Halifax. It wasn't the degree that excited her so much as her desire to visit her grandmother's grave so she could say to her, "We've come full circle." She used to accompany her grandmother when she cleaned the big homes not far from the university. Bev's illness prevented her from attending convocation.

She had prepared her speech before her health took an unexpected turn. As we had done in the past, she shared her speech with me, the speech she would never deliver. Students and those who would be attending convocation would miss her words of wisdom. I read the speech aloud to her. This would be the last time we would talk about a speech she wrote. I promised her that I would someday publicly read her speech.

"You liked it?" she asked.

"Yes, very much," I said. "I look forward to sharing it someday."

She smiled and gave me a nod.

Soon it was time for me to head to the airport. I kissed her goodbye. Still in denial that she was dying, I said, "Bev, I'll see you soon. I'll be back to spend more time with you."

She looked at me and smiled. I turned and left.

Beverly died on May 16, 2001, two days after I returned to Halifax. I attended her private funeral on May 19. I kept my promise, and with her husband's permission, I read the convocation speech she would have delivered at Mount Saint Vincent University. Her public memorial service took place on May 30, 2001, at the Toronto Centre for the Arts.

When I returned home to Halifax after Bev's funeral I felt lost. My dear and true friend was gone, and I was still grieving the loss of my mother, who had died five months earlier. My family suggested that I act on getting a cat, something I had been procrastinating. One day when I was heading to work, I met the superintendent of my building. He said he remembered my talking about some day getting a cat. He told me that one of my neighbours had a cat that was a special breed he had not heard of before. He said the cat was beautiful and he was certain they would be happy to introduce me to their cat. I asked what the breed was. He said, "Ragdoll." My mind flashed back to my time with Beverly when I was preoccupied with her doll.

I did my research, met my neighbour's cat, and I knew this was the breed I wanted. When I visited the breeder I was amazed

In 2008, Mayann Francis (right) received an honorary Doctor of Humane Letters from Mount Saint Vincent University in Halifax. The convocation was attended by her brother-in-law Vincent Waterman and her sister Isabel.
(MOUNT SAINT VINCENT UNIVERSITY)

to see so many Ragdolls. After she interviewed me, she said she had a new litter born on May 9. That was the very day that Bev had informed me of her pending death. When I told the breeder this, she said she would make certain she selected a special kitten from that litter.

A week prior to the adoption, I was flying back to Halifax from a business trip to Cape Breton. I was dozing when the flight attendant announced we would be landing shortly. Then I heard a voice say, "Call her Angel." I looked at the people in my immediate vicinity to see if anyone had spoken. To my surprise they were either dozing like I had been or looking out the window. I dismissed what I had heard, or thought I heard.

On the drive home from the airport, Beverly's memorial service flashed in front of me. Fortunately, I was not driving. "A Tribute to an Angel" was the theme for the service. I had also called Beverly my angel when I delivered my acceptance speech at the Harry Jerome Awards. I named my Ragdoll cat Angel. She was my comforter and companion for fourteen years. When my beautiful Angel died, a mutual friend of mine and Bev's said, "Angel was the last connection to Beverly."

An honorary Doctor of Humane Letters was awarded to Beverly posthumously, in the fall of 2001. Emerson accepted the award. In 2008, I would receive the same honour as Bev from Mount Saint Vincent. I could not help but think that somehow Bev had something to do with my receiving this honour. Her spirit was with me as I walked across the stage.

I cannot explain the series of events that occurred—the ragdoll, my beloved cat, receiving honorary degrees from the same universities, or my experience on the airplane. There are some things that simply cannot be explained.

Beverly taught me many life lessons that I carry with me every day. I believe her spirit is with me. With her husband's blessing, I devoted this chapter to my friend Bev. I now close it with the unedited speech my friend and mentor would have delivered at Mount Saint Vincent University convocation in the spring of 2001. Once you finish this chapter and her speech you will understand why, in the words of Maya Angelou, my dear friend was a "phenomenal woman." And I miss her.

MOUNT SAINT VINCENT UNIVERSITY CONVOCATION SPEECH, MAY 11, 2001
BY BEVERLY MASCOLL

President Brown, Chancellor Brink, members of the Governing Council, graduates, families, ladies and gentlemen.

As I prepared to come here today I realized that life has brought me full circle.

It all started just a short distance from here where I grew up in Fall River. It was in Fall River that my grandmother prepared me for many of life's little lessons such as caring, sharing, and the stamina to survive when the going gets tough.

In my most ambitious dreams, I never expected that I would one day be here at Mount Saint Vincent University receiving an honorary degree.

As an entrepreneur, it's a proud moment, because Mount Saint Vincent is dedicated to the education of women, and the Centre for Women in Business is meeting the needs of the growing number of women entrepreneurs.

For a number of years I worked as an executive assistant in the general market beauty industry. There was a void in the Canadian market. No one was filling the specialized hair care needs for women of colour, and that's when I decided to become an entrepreneur. I understood the business, a key factor for any entrepreneur who wants to succeed.

The necessary support that exists for women entrepreneurs today was non-existent when I started. When financial institutions turned me down, many times all I had to rely on were those little lessons learned from my grandmother and how she taught me to survive when the going gets rough (and the going can get rough). Those lessons established a belief in myself and my commitment to being successful.

Today we celebrate you as you graduate and make your commitment to being successful. It was just about this time last year I also graduated from university. I received my BA in Women's Studies from York University in June 2000. The day-to-day interaction with students and the joy of learning was a gratifying experience. Many times in tutorial when we talked about history, for me, it was often current events. Just the frame of reference differed.

Most of my life experience was learned in what they call the "real world." I am here to tell you what you've just gone through—a few years in another part of the real world, essays, and finals—is very real. Reflect on the experiences you've had over the past few years in university, because you've also learned some lessons you'll refer to as you travel down the road of life.

It's been said that every time you graduate, you move on and there are more people to know, more difficult jobs to do, more experiences to have than you have yet gone through. One of the things that graduation says is that you are now ready. A few years ago you, today's grads, made a commitment to obtaining a Mount Saint Vincent degree, and you have accomplished that goal.

Life requires commitment. Let me say that again, and if you only hear one thing today, hear this: "Life requires commitment."

Don't let other people tell you what you can and cannot accomplish.

I was often told that I was crazy because, after all, what could a poor Black girl from Nova Scotia contribute to the cosmetic industry?

But I had something that was priceless. I believed that I could accomplish whatever I set out to do. If you want something you've never had before, you have to be prepared to do something you've never done before. I understood the power of believing in myself.

Be honest about your motivation to achieve. If you conduct your lives honestly and honourably, not expediently, you can achieve real fulfilment.

It is also important that at the end of the day you can look back at your life with few regrets.

In life you have one of two things: discipline or regret. I asked a very dear friend whether she had any regrets as she looked back on her life. You know what she said?

"I wish I cried more;

"I wish I laughed more; I wish I loved more;

"I wish I sang out loud at the top of my lungs; I wish I danced in the rain;

"I wish I read more books;

"I wish I told people dear to me how I really felt, and once, just once, I would like to jump, without looking, to truly feel the wind beneath my wings."

All of you have reached a tremendous milestone in your lives, one that you can be very proud of. With your graduation, you now join a prestigious group of Mount Saint Vincent alumni. It took courage, commitment, and dedication to get you this far, and it will take courage, commitment, and dedication to take you where you would like to go.

In closing I would like to leave you with the wisdom of author Langston Hughes: "If you never say the words I cannot, you will never have to say the words I did not."

Chapter 7

FROM TORONTO TO HALIFAX

*For I am about to do something new. See, I have already
begun! Do you not see it? I will make a pathway through
the wilderness. I will create rivers in the dry wasteland.*

ISAIAH 43:19

My mother was still living with Isabel in Sydney when
I moved back to Halifax in 1999. Mother's dive into
dementia was increasing. I went home to Whitney Pier
to give my sister a break. It was difficult to see my mother this way.
Here was a woman who took pride in everything she did. After
my father's death in 1982, she seemed lost and lonely. She had
lived for over forty years with the man she loved, who took care of
everything. When he died we had to teach my mom how to write
a cheque. Even though we were not rich, my father made certain
before he died that all bills were paid, and everything, including
funeral arrangements for both my parents, were clearly outlined
in my dad's will.

My mom was not the type to go out and find new friends. My sister wanted her to join a seniors' club, but Mom was not having any of this. We are fortunate that she always knew who we were. My brother Howard would often spend time with her and make her laugh. She also had a cat that was very protective of her. He would sit on the bed with her and refuse to move until he was good and ready.

Soon we became the parents and Mom became the child. Through it all, there was something deep inside that caused her to keep her pride. Whenever I told her it was time to go to the washroom, there were tears in her eyes. I would kiss her and tell her it was okay, that I loved her and it was now our turn to take care of her. I will never forget my sister's phone call on December 3, 2000, informing me that our mother had died in her sleep. I was at a United Way Centraide board meeting in Ottawa when the call came. It hit me like a ton of bricks that now both my parents were gone. I felt depressed and alone. After a period of time and prayer, I realized that no matter where I journey, my parents' spirit will always be with me. I was ready to begin another chapter. I wanted them to be proud of me because they had given me the foundation to stand and grow.

I have been fortunate in my career with the many opportunities presented to me. Sometimes I was nervous about walking through a door of opportunity, but I conquered those fears and went forward. My faith played a great role in giving me the confidence I needed to face something new and challenging.

In the final year of PMETS's three-year mandate, I was contacted by a headhunting firm hired by the Province of Nova Scotia to recruit a CEO for the Nova Scotia Human Rights Commission. Interestingly, a few days before the call, someone who had seen the advertisement in the paper suggested I take a look and apply. My Toronto friends, including my dear friend Beverly, encouraged me to apply. They said, "We do not want to see you leave Toronto, but this is a great opportunity. Go for it."

I went through several interviews, including a rigorous panel interview. In his letter of congratulations when he heard I was offered the position, one of my references, Dr. Howard Clark, former president of Dalhousie University, wrote this:

> I was not asked to write a letter of reference for you...instead someone from the consultant's office called me by phone and grilled me for at least three-quarters of an hour. It was very thorough. By the end of it, I told the caller that I had worked hard enough to be given the position myself. It was easily the most extensive, well-organized, and penetrating phone reference I have ever been asked to give, and I was quite impressed by it. So you can be very certain that you thoroughly deserve the appointment and that the search was very competently done.

I knew I would miss the friends I had made during my time in Toronto, and I was grateful that I'd had the opportunity to work with the Ontario government. Nonetheless, I was ready to try living in Halifax once again. Returning home as director and CEO of the Nova Scotia Human Rights Commission would give me the chance to make positive changes in the area of social justice. I knew the lessons I learned both at PMETS and the OWD would assist me in my new role in Nova Scotia.

I was appointed director in 1999 by an Order in Council and on the recommendation of Robert S. Harrison, the attorney general, minister of justice responsible for the administration of the Human Rights Act. And on June 9, 1999, he introduced me to the House of Assembly. To be in the legislature and welcomed by its members was a proud and emotional moment for me. One of the parties stressed that I was a non-partisan appointment. Apparently, I was joining the commission at a time when there was controversy about partisan board appointments. The commission was also experiencing internal challenges. I knew I had my work cut out for me.

I found it hard to believe that I was now responsible for the agency that protected the rights of citizens who are discriminated against under the Human Rights Act. The commission was established in 1967 with the mandate to challenge discrimination on the basis of race, religion, and ethnic background. The first executive director, Marvin Schiff, served from 1968 to 1971, followed by Dr. George McCurdy, the first Black person to serve in this capacity, which he did from 1971 to 1983. I was fortunate to have worked under Dr. McCurdy's leadership when I first joined the commission as a human rights officer in 1972. Dr. McCurdy was a great inspiration and role model, strong, determined, and committed to fighting for human rights. He took a personal interest in the development of human rights officers and encouraged us to take advantage of the many opportunities to learn and develop investigation skills through educational conferences and training programs.

Under McCurdy, commission offices were opened in New Glasgow, Digby, and Sydney. In a book written to commemorate the commission's twenty-fifth anniversary, Dr. Bridglal Pachai (executive director from 1989 to 1994) writes,

> During [McCurdy's] tenure, he was also responsible for the introduction of the concepts of: Affirmative Action in Employment to major employers in the private as well as public sectors; Educational Programs on Human Rights Education in the Public School System; [and] Municipal Affirmative Action Committees involving hundreds of Nova Scotians in the voluntary promotion of human rights.

I credit much of what I have learned in my approach to human rights to George McCurdy. He helped me hone my investigative and negotiating skills, which I have used not only in my professional life, but also in my personal life. I can still remember watching Dr.

McCurdy negotiate a settlement. He was firm, polite, knowledgeable, strategic, and successful. He was a great teacher. As a leader in the field of human rights in this province and in Canada, he raised the profile of the commission. In my view his efforts and dedication formed the foundation of the commission's approach to human rights in Nova Scotia.

When I assumed the role of director and chief executive officer of the Nova Scotia Human Rights Commission on August 3, 1999, I did so under a Liberal government. That same year the government was defeated. John Hamm's Progressive Conservative party became the government. I had had a similar experience in Ontario. Within a short period of assuming my role there, the NDP government, under Bob Rae, was defeated by the Conservative government led by Mike Harris.

The Human Rights Commission (HRC) is an independent agency of government. Commissioners are appointed by the government through an application process and are responsible for making decisions about human rights cases. The minister of justice is responsible for the Human Rights Act. The late Michael Baker, the Conservatives' attorney general and minister of justice, was a wonderful person to work with. He very rarely missed any of the events organized by the commission. This was very important: staff and the public could see that the minister responsible for the Act took human rights in this province seriously. Minister Baker was not only intelligent, he was a keen listener, asked the right questions, and understood and respected the independence of the commission.

Returning to Halifax for the second time felt much different than when I first returned home in 1990. I felt my time in Toronto had prepared me for my eventual return to the province. When I first returned home after having been in New York for sixteen years, I was disappointed in what I did not see. I did not see people of colour working in prominent places. Toronto filled that void.

Even though I had only been in Toronto for less than five years, when I returned to Halifax in 1999, I saw a slight movement in diversity. I was shocked, thrilled, and pleased when I saw a Muslim woman wearing a hijab. Then I saw a Black woman working in a retail store. Again I was pleased. Only one, but there she was. Now I had a cautious hope that things would change for the better when it came to an inclusive society in the province of my birth.

When I took over as agency head, there was a backlog of cases, high-profile complaints that were receiving media attention, and low staff morale. The commission was once seen as a leader in the field of human rights. By 1999 its reputation was tarnished as a result of a series of events both internal and external. It was obvious to me that if the commission was to effect change, we had to get our own house in order.

One of the first things I did was to initiate a comprehensive organizational review, the first since the commission was created. The review meant taking a hard look at current practices and resources and making sure they matched the external climate. When the commission was first established, the intention was to help combat discrimination against marginalized communities, such as African Nova Scotians and Aboriginals. Since its inception, the Human Rights Act has, of course, been expanded. Decades after its inception, we needed to ask the question, "Was the commission doing the job well enough for the external environment that had changed so rapidly?" This review was important if the commission was to remain relevant.

In addition to the review, it was important both to raise the commission's profile and to expel any myths the public or staff might hold about a Black woman as CEO. Having been in various management roles and sat at many management tables as the only Black person, I was well aware of the attitude some people held. The attitude of low expectations for Black people is often on a subconscious level and can be traced back to the days of slavery. I knew that being in this high-profile position presented the challenge of being judged not only as an individual but also as a proxy for all Black men and women.

I decided to make many public appearances. I did not want the public to view the commission with fear. Instead I wanted them to understand and respect the work of the commission. I used every opportunity to address various communities about human rights and to educate people about the commission and its work. I wanted people to see the commission not only as an enforcement agency, but also as an organization that can be used to learn about "isms" and how a more welcoming climate, with zero tolerance for violations of the human rights code, can be created by an organization or community or workplace. I believed that education about racism and discrimination was extremely important when it came to race relations and that if we were to thrive economically, we had to ensure that overt and institutionalized racism and discrimination did not prevent citizens from having equal access to opportunities.

As head of the Human Rights Commission, there were many positive opportunities that brought a smile to my lips. In 2000, a year after I left Toronto, I was invited back to Toronto by a friend who was one of the organizers for Archbishop Desmond Tutu's visit to the city. I was fortunate to be a head-table guest at a dinner in his honour. I was also part of his entourage for the awarding of his honorary degree from Osgoode Hall Law School.

I will never forget a brief conversation with Desmond Tutu. When he learned where I was from, he spoke very highly about Nova Scotia. With a smile on his face, he mentioned his introduction to and fondness of Jack Daniels. I quickly responded with something like, "Oh yes, I know him." I knew the name was familiar and I was certain I must have met Mr. Daniels. Then there was silence. The archbishop looked at me and laughed. It did not take me long to realize he had been referring to Jack Daniel's Tennessee Whiskey.

On October 3, 2002, I was invited to the Pictou County Chamber of Commerce to share my vision with business leaders and community and cultural groups. My presentation was hosted by Kimberly-Clarke Nova Scotia as a result of the company's diversity program. In the presentation, an excerpt of which I'll share here, I stressed the importance and value of a diverse workforce if our society is to prosper.

> *Surely we have become smart enough in this new century to realize that racism, sexism, classism, and all those other "isms" are not only a moral blemish on our society, but they also harm all of us by diminishing our well-being on the social and economic level. If we do not solve the problems of discrimination, can any of us say we have a bright future? Truly successful communities and companies are only possible in the absence of discrimination. Human rights must be everyone's business. Business and government have looked for ways to reduce red tape in order to promote business growth. I am sure for some business and community leaders, human rights is viewed as part of that red tape. My message to you is that human rights is actually a key to a competitive advantage for business, and therefore a key to healthier communities. Human rights work at every level of society to remove the barriers that prevent citizens from contributing to the economic and social development of our province.*

My faith prompted me to reach out to faith leaders as I believed they had a role to play in fostering healthy communities. I started a program called Day of Reflection for religious leaders. The first Day of Reflection: Spirit of Community was held on November 9, 2001. I invited religious leaders from different faiths to the Red Room in Province House. The leaders had an opportunity to dialogue with each other during breakfast. After they were settled in their assigned seats, there was a moment of quiet reflection, followed by a sharing of what the spirit of community meant to them. The minister of justice, Michael Baker, attended as did the Honourable Myra Freeman, lieutenant-governor, who proclaimed the Day of Reflection. Many relationships developed among the religious leaders. During my tenure, I held this special day once a year. Many if not all of the leaders recognized that they had a role to play in fighting injustice. I challenged them to take action.

In addition to the annual Day of Reflection, I accepted invitations from a variety of religious organizations and their places of worship to speak to them about human rights and social justice.

I continued to raise the profile of the commission when I accepted an invitation from the *Halifax Herald* to contribute a regular column. The commission was also invited to make a presentation to the Senate of Canada. On November 26, 2001, James E. Dewar, chairperson of the Nova Scotia Commission, and I made our presentation to the Senate Committee on Human Rights, talking about the history of the Nova Scotia Human Rights Commission and the work we were doing. We stressed the importance of reaching out to the public, businesses, and government to discuss the importance of human rights if we are to have a society where everyone feels welcome and has equal opportunity to jobs, housing, education, and economic development. Among other things, we talked about Parliament having an expanded and positive role with international human rights through education and said that we felt international human rights conventions should be playing a more prominent role in public debate. It was a privilege to appear before the committee.

There were several high-profile cases that thrust the commission onto the national stage. The Kirk Johnson racial profiling case, "Driving while Black," received national and international attention. At the time of the incident in April 1998, Mr. Johnson, a boxer from North Preston, was a resident of Texas. He and his cousin were pursued along Highway 111 and eventually stopped at a shopping plaza in Dartmouth by the Halifax Regional Police Service. The police officer was not satisfied with the valid Texas documentation provided by Mr. Johnson's cousin, who was driving Mr. Johnson's car. His cousin was ticketed and Mr. Johnson's vehicle was towed. Mr. Johnson filed a complaint with the commission alleging that he was pulled over because he was Black and that the incident was an example of racial profiling. The Nova Scotia Human Rights Commission Board of Inquiry found that the Halifax Regional Police had discriminated against Mr. Johnson. Two other high-profile cases were the breastfeeding case, where a mother was asked by the owner of a store not to breastfeed her baby while in her store; and the sexual orientation case, where a female schoolteacher was dismissed after being falsely accused of having an affair with a female student. The Board of Inquiry found in the commission's favour in all three cases. As the face of the commission, I had to be prepared to answer the many questions from media and the public.

In the course of my career I have learned that every organization must take a hard look at itself on a regular basis to ensure that its mandate and operations are keeping pace with the world around it. This includes ensuring that there are educational opportunities available for staff to continually upgrade their skills. It means consulting with staff not only from the top down but from the ground up as well. Whenever there is a review it is important that staff are kept in the loop.

Communications becomes very important. I held a series of relaxed breakfast meetings with staff, giving them an opportunity to freely express their comments and ideas for solutions to problems. I wanted them to express their views respectfully and without fear. Not everyone participated in these breakfasts, and that was okay. I saw my role as creating opportunities for sharing. I made certain that updates on the change process were communicated regularly at staff meetings. I also had an open-door policy.

During my time at the commission, I was asked by the government to be the ombudsman for six months, the time expected to fill the position. I was surprised when asked because there was a highly qualified and respected person performing the role. It is sometimes a mystery why and how government decisions are made. The ombudsman's term had concluded and his contract was not being renewed, so I was asked to assume the role on a short-term basis. I was completely taken by surprise because as head of the commission, I would be in a conflict of interest situation. Plus, I did not think the public would be happy with the government's decision.

The role of the ombudsman is to investigate maladministration on the part of government departments. How could the ombudsman's office investigate the Human Rights Commission if the head of both organizations was the same person? Would the public believe that I would have nothing to do with any complaints involving the commission or ombudsman's office? These were serious questions. Nonetheless, the government proceeded with the appointment.

Systems were immediately put in place by lawyers for the ombudsman's office that would ensure none of the files of complaints involving either that office or the commission could or would be seen by me. This was a comprehensive procedure. The problem was how to convince the public that I would not see the files or influence an investigation.

Added to this challenge, some members of the Black community could not understand why I did not refuse the government's request. Someone said to me, "You could have said no." You see, the ombudsman whose contract was not renewed was a member of the Black community, Douglas Ruck. He was deeply respected by the Black community and beyond. I also held him in high regard. He understood the position in which I was placed. He was supportive of my decision and gave me words of encouragement. I could not have moved forward with this new challenge if it were not for his wise counsel. He is the true measure of a decent man. He moved on with his life and continued to be successful.

The projected six months turned out to be two years. My faith in God, my true friends, and staff at both the commission and the ombudsman's office helped me weather a turbulent time.

I was working at the ombudsman's office the morning I received word that my friend Beverly had died. My executive secretary at the Human Rights Commission received the call. She left the commission office and walked to the office of the ombudsman several streets away to break the news to me personally. I will always be grateful for her decision to do this. Had I been in the commission office and answered the phone call about my friend's death, I am not certain how I would have reacted.

While at the commission, I was fortunate to complete a project that began when I lived in Toronto. As a board member of the United Way Centraide Canada (UW), I was co-chair of a major international project. The International Advisory Committee for Capacity Building in the Voluntary Sector: Collaborative Learning in Brazilian and Canadian Organizations project began in 1997 and concluded in 2003. This was a fantastic opportunity for which I will always be grateful. Being exposed to the challenges of a major international project encouraged me to develop my facilitation and management skills. Working with the Brazilian project team enhanced my personal development on cultural differences. If you ever have an opportunity to take part in an international project, conquer your fear and take the plunge. You not only grow professionally but personally. In her thank you letter to me, dated April 17, 2003, the project manager said: "Our Brazilian colleagues were provided with a model of leadership that was respectful of their culture and priorities, without losing sight of Canadian perspectives." When you understand and respect the culture of the country you are working with, chances are your project will be successful.

My time at the commission ended abruptly in the summer of 2006 when I was named the next lieutenant-governor of Nova Scotia. Once the announcement was made, I had to resign as CEO and executive director. I was extremely happy to have been named lieutenant-governor, but I felt my work at the commission was not finished. Nonetheless, I took comfort in knowing that gains had been made: the raised profile of the commission; success in a number of high-profile cases; an organizational review that yielded positive results; implementation of mediation services; and enhanced education about the commission, human rights, racism, and discrimination. It was my hope that whoever succeeded me would build on what was accomplished and continue the change process to create a strong and vibrant commission that works for all Nova Scotians.

Mayann Francis as a toddler "cutting her eyes" on the steps of her Hankard Street home in the Whitney Pier area of Sydney, Nova Scotia.
(COURTESY OF AUTHOR)

Mayann Francis's father, George Anthony Francis, was the pastor of St. Philip's African Orthodox Church in Sydney, Nova Scotia, for over forty years, from 1940 to his death in 1982. This painting hangs today in St. Philip's African Orthodox Church. (COURTESY OF AUTHOR)

Growing up, Mayann Francis had clothes for school, clothes to play in, and Sunday clothes. Here she stands in the living room of her Sydney home, dressed for church.

(COURTESY OF AUTHOR)

Mayann Francis tried her hand at many things—including modelling—during her time in New York in the 1970s.

(COURTESY OF AUTHOR)

In May 2006, Prime Minister Stephen Harper asked Mayann Francis to be the thirty-first lieutenant-governor of Nova Scotia. (PHOTO BY DEB RANSOM)

On September 7, 2006, Mayann Francis was installed as Nova Scotia's lieutenant-governor. Here, she signs the installation papers as Premier Rodney MacDonald (left) and Chief Justice Michael MacDonald look on. (PROVINCE OF NOVA SCOTIA)

Lieutenant-Governor Mayann Francis delivers the Speech from the Throne on March 31, 2011. (PROVINCE OF NOVA SCOTIA)

Members of the Nova Scotia legislature listen attentively as Lieutenant-Governor Mayann Francis delivers the Speech from the Throne on March 31, 2011.
(PROVINCE OF NOVA SCOTIA)

Lieutenant-Governor Mayann Francis accompanies Queen Elizabeth II as she leaves Government House at the conclusion of the royal visit to Halifax in 2010.
(PROVINCE OF NOVA SCOTIA)

Mayann Francis adopted her beloved cat, Noah, on December 29, 2016. (COURTESY OF AUTHOR)

Lieutenant-Governor Mayann Francis's personal coat of arms. The sugar cane represents her Caribbean ancestry, the bald eagles allude to her Cape Breton roots, and the cat represents Angel, her beloved pet. The Spanish motto, a nod to her father's first language, means "knowledge, truth, love, and justice."
(COURTESY OF AUTHOR)

Lieutenant-Governor Mayann Francis's aides-de-camp were volunteers from the RCMP, Halifax Regional Police, and from the army, navy, and air force. This photo was taken during an event at Government House. (PROVINCE OF NOVA SCOTIA)

A historic moment: Canada's first Black governor general, Michaëlle Jean, and Nova Scotia's first Black lieutenant-governor, Mayann Francis, meet for the first fime at Nova Scotia's Black Cultural Centre in February 2007. (PROVINCE OF NOVA SCOTIA)

Chapter 8

MAKING HISTORY

For I know the plans I have for you. They are plans for
good and not for disaster, to give you a future and a hope.
JEREMIAH 29:11

M y executive assistant ran back to his office, which was
connected to my office. I heard Michael apologize for
disconnecting Mr. Penner, director of appointments for
the Prime Minister's Office (PMO). "Ms. Francis is available to speak
with you. I will connect you." I realized he was not joking.

I had an intense and mysterious conversation with Mr. Penner,
who did not reveal why he was calling. I answered all of his questions and, at his request, sent him an updated CV the next day. I
might add that he was already familiar with my background. He
thoroughly impressed me; he did not give any hint as to why he
called or why he wanted my CV. His final words were that I might
be called to Ottawa to meet the Prime Minister. I was speechless.

When our conversation ended, my assistant and secretary
rushed into my office. We tried to figure out why the PMO would

call me. I was so nervous, I foolishly said, "I always file my taxes. And I know I did not do anything wrong." A few days later Mr. Penner called and asked that I book a flight to Ottawa to meet with the Prime Minister.

Normally when I fly I select an aisle seat. This time I requested a window seat because I knew that the hour and day I was flying out, there was a strong chance that I would meet someone I knew who might ask why I was flying to Ottawa. My instincts were correct. So I kept my dark glasses on and my head down for the entire flight. I also took my time leaving the plane when we landed. You see, I am not good at telling fibs.

The next day, May 30, 2006, I met Mr. Penner, who escorted me to Prime Minister Stephen Harper's office. I was in such a state of shock. I tried my best to remain calm and to answer intelligently any questions he might ask. The little Black girl from Whitney Pier was meeting with the leader of our great country.

When I left the prime minister's office, I was not certain if I would take the opportunity he offered. I could not help but remember the unfounded negative reaction to the appointment of Michaëlle Jean as governor general just one year earlier, in 2005. And of course, I was fully aware of past and current race relations in Nova Scotia. I did not know how people, including staff of the lieutenant-governor's office and government, would react to having a Black woman as their lieutenant-governor.

Mr. Penner understood my feelings. He was, however, confident that the majority of people would respond positively to my appointment because of my education, reputation, experience, and background and that I was qualified to fill the post.

When I returned to my hotel room, I was confused and afraid. Before I went to sleep, I asked Mary and God for guidance. The next morning I phoned Mr. Penner. And the rest, as they say, is history.

Under our parliamentary system, the prime minister's recommendations for lieutenant-governors are presented to the governor general for appointment. (For governor general appointments, the recommendation is made by the prime minister directly to Her Majesty.) I am not certain how I came to the prime minister's attention. I will be forever thankful for the trust Mr. Harper had in me. And I am grateful to the person(s) who put my name forth for this privileged opportunity. It was a defining moment not only for me, but for history as well. The first Black governor general in the history of this country appointed me as the first Black lieutenant-governor of Nova Scotia and only the second Black lieutenant-governor appointed to this role in Canadian history.

Six and a half years earlier, on December 17, 1999, I attended a party at the home of my two close friends, Bernard Burton and Michael Noonan. With the new century only a few weeks away, Bernie asked his guests to write our wishes for the twenty-first century. He provided us with paper and envelopes. Without revealing what we wrote, we placed our responses in the envelope, which we dated and sealed. He told us he would put them in a safe place and return them to us in ten years.

On December 31, 2009, Bernie and Michael brought my envelope to Government House. I had forgotten about that December night. When I opened the envelope, the look on my face prompted Bernie to ask what I had written. I could not speak or move. He took the paper from me.

"My goodness," he said. "Wow."

For a moment we sat in silence. Then we smiled. This is what I had written: "That I will be able to motivate people to positive action through my motivational talks. That people celebrate and embrace differences. That peace and love win over hate. As Lt.-Governor for the province of Nova Scotia, my positive actions and my determination to build NS as a model province is realized."

Less than seven years later, on September 7, 2006, I was sworn in as the thirty-first lieutenant-governor of Nova Scotia, the first Black person and only the second woman to be appointed to this prestigious role. I followed the Honourable Myra Freeman, the thirtieth lieutenant-governor and first woman to hold this title.

When I lived in New York and Ontario people frequently asked me what would bring me back to Nova Scotia. I said, "A position with deputy minister status and/or lieutenant-governor." This was a joke. I knew it was wishful thinking. Plus, at the time, I was not interested in returning to Nova Scotia. Sometimes our life takes a turn we do not expect. In 1999 I was appointed head of the Human Rights Commission with deputy head status, and in 2006 I became lieutenant-governor. Just like my experience with Beverly's ragdoll and my beloved Ragdoll cat, Angel, I cannot explain the above premonitions.

When the announcement was made that I would be the thirty-first lieutenant-governor of Nova Scotia, you can imagine the media and public flurry. In the mist of this exciting news, I think it was a day after the announcement, the US Consul General in Halifax paid me a visit at the Nova Scotia Human Rights Commission. There was concern that my appointment as lieu-tenant-governor would somehow conflict with my American citizen-ship. It was clear to me that there was a lack of understanding of the vice-regal role and responsibilities. As you know, unlike the role of lieutenant-governor in Canada, in the United States lieutenant-gov-ernor is an elected position, a political role that might influence policy decisions. Officials in the United States did an expedited investigation about my case and determined that my appointment would not be in conflict with my American citizenship. If the oppo-site had been determined, I am sure I would have had to make a very difficult decision. Thank heavens I was lieutenant-governor and am still proud to still hold my American citizenship.

In his congratulatory email dated August 23, 2006, my dear friend, professor and author Dr. Cecil Foster, wrote,

I cannot help but to think that your father, Marcus Garvey, George McGuire, Padmore, Malcolm X, and all the departed African elders (especially those with West Indian backgrounds) are having quite a discussion over your appointment. Indeed, your father might rightly claim to have foretold an occasion like this with the name he and your mom chose for you. It is the special way you have taught me to pronounce it, so that your name comes out as a variation of Ma(r)yam—who, as you know, in African orthodoxy is the saint of Ethiopia (usually a reference for Africa in the Bible), the mother of the God the redeemer, the mother of the nation, the mediatrix. When "Myann" (where a double n sounds like an m) becomes the L-G on September 7, all the elders will be at Province House; they will be beside themselves with glee that you are, indeed, symbolically the mother and sovereign of the Nova Scotian nation, at least, representing the symbolic mother and sovereign of the commonwealth (including all those nations in Africa and the Caribbean); they will be congratulating your dad for his vision and prophecy—and the gift in the person and name that he gave to all us Africans.

When I read his email, chills went through my body. I do recall teaching him how to pronounce my name. He is the only person who pronounces my name this way. I was not aware of my name's history until his email.

My 1999 prediction, Cecil Foster's research, my middle name (Elizabeth, after Her Majesty), my conditions for returning to live in Nova Scotia—all conspired to lead me to firmly believe that God's plan for me was realized when I became lieutenant-governor.

Throughout my career, I was frequently the first Black person to perform certain roles. While it was always an honour to break down barriers so others could follow, the pressure of being the first Black in any circumstance was a major challenge. I knew I carried

Black men and women on my shoulders. When I was sworn in, I said in my installation speech that I wanted "my appointment to be seen as a sign of hope for anyone who believed they had been oppressed or denied opportunity."

After I was sworn in as lieutenant-governor, I called the first Black lieutenant-governor in Canada, Lincoln Alexander, who served from 1985 to 1991 in Ontario. We had a great conversation and he gave me sage advice. A couple of things he said stayed with me. He told me that when my term ended, I should disappear for a while to give my successor space. He also advised me not to accept invitations where my successor would be. He said I should remember that the premier works for the lieutenant-governor. He apparently told Bob Rae, "You are the premier but I am the lieutenant-governor. In short, I'm your boss." He told me never to forget this.

The three of us—Lincoln Alexander, Michaëlle Jean, and myself—broke the colour barrier for Black people by joining the elite and exclusive club once reserved for white males. To paraphrase Maya Angelou's "Still I Rise," "[We are] the dream and the hope of the slave." In a public lecture I gave in 2016, I said the following:

> *Slavery had such a negative impact on society. It was one of the most frighteningly powerful and cruel institutions because it permeated every aspect of the life of countless generations of Black men and women. So powerful was the institution that centuries later, the legacy it created still haunts Black men, women, and youth here in Canada and throughout the diaspora, because it succeeded in convincing the world that Black people were inferior and lazy. The three of us smashed the glass ceiling, dispelling those long held beliefs still in the minds of some people.*

Discrimination and racism do not take vacations. They can rear their ugly heads anywhere and anytime. There are people who are overtly racist, people who have unconscious biases, and people who practise polite, hidden racism. When I was welcoming guests to Province House for one of my first official functions, a white man who was shaking my hand said, "We've had good lieutenant-governors. I hope you will be too." The look on his face and the tone of his voice clearly demonstrated his low expectations of me.

Throughout my career, I knew if I did not perform well in any of the positions I held, my actions would jeopardize the possibility of another Black person being hired. The discussion around the boardroom table or in human resources would go something like this: "We tried, it just did not work out. She did not fit in."

As lieutenant-governor, I knew the pressure would be greater than what I experienced in the past. Being the first Black person appointed to anything raises the question in the minds of some people whether the appointment was based on merit and qualifications or was because of race. Take for example an article that appeared in the *Cape Breton Post* on January 8, 2012, a few months prior to the conclusion of my tenure, written by Chris Shannon:

> *Cape Breton University political professor David Johnson said the prime minister could very well choose a non-partisan to fill the role. He said he'll be looking for Harper to name someone of the same 'calibre' as the current Gov. Gen. David Johnson. Harper may feel less pressure to appoint a woman due to Francis and her immediate predecessor, Myra Freeman, Johnson said. There is somewhat less pressure on any federal government to use the appointment to demonstrate affinity with the values of affirmative action.*

Was he implying that Prime Minister Harper's selection was based on affirmative action and/or partisanship? Was he implying that my appointment was not based on merit and that I was not qualified to perform the duties of the role? Did he believe that I had performed poorly in my previous role? Were his comments an evaluation and a commentary on my performance while I was in office, and did he feel compelled to offer advice to the prime minister on the calibre of the next appointee? Did he feel the prime minister made a mistake when he selected me? If the answer to any of these questions is yes, then I would suggest that his thinking is an insult not only to me but to Mr. Harper as well.

I contrast his remarks with comments from Mr. Leroy Peach of Port Morien in a letter he wrote to Her Majesty in August 2008. Mr. Peach was informing Her Majesty that his community was being presented with the Lieutenant-Governor Community Spirit Award, which I had created in 2007 to recognize efforts to build positive relationships that contribute to quality of life, primarily in rural communities. In part this is what he wrote about the award and about me.

> *This award was created to recognize communities for their efforts toward improvement for their citizens as well as to celebrate all that has gone on in areas in years past. This lady has been out among us, listening to our concerns, answering our questions, and interacting with us on a very personal level. I think she is the type of person the Monarchy had in mind when the position was created. Not only is she representative to the people, but also of the people. As long as people such as her are chosen to fill these roles, the Monarchy will retain its position of admiration and respect in the hearts of Canadians, and particularly, Maritime Canadians.*

Thank you, Mr. Peach. And yes thank you, Professor Johnson, because your comments validated what I suspected some people were thinking. It is important to know people's views. We live in a democracy and people are free to express their opinions, even when they are insulting and demeaning.

Regardless of what some people may have been thinking about my appointment, I accepted the call to duty and the call to serve my province and country. For me, the role of the lieutenant-governor was a call to service, which I did not enter into lightly. Instead, as I said in my installation speech, "I approach my new role soberly by appreciating the dignity and honour that the role requires. My solemn pledge is to always serve to the best of my abilities and to always uphold the respect that the office deserves." I held my father's Bible and pledged my allegiance.

I could not imagine taking the oath of office without first spending time with God. On the morning of my installation, I began the day with prayer and reflection at a special service at the Cathedral Church of All Saints in Halifax. I wanted God's blessing on my new appointment and to offer my thanks for this great honour. Bishop Fredrick James Hiltz, who went on to become the Primate of the Anglican Church of Canada in 2007, presided over the service. I invited faith leaders from different religious backgrounds to take part in the service. I was grateful for everyone who attended and joined in the service of thanksgiving and blessing.

I also wanted the public to join with me in this special service—and they did. It was standing room only at the Cathedral. In a few hours I would be the Queen's representative. I wanted to serve the people of Nova Scotia, and it was important that they start the journey with me. Within a few months of my installation I realized that the people of this province would be my strength throughout my tenure. They, along with my faith in God, gave me the hope I needed to keep going.

My installation was not only historic, but it was also special for Whitney Pier, the small community where I was born and raised. The Oath of Office was administered by the Chief Justice of Nova Scotia, the Honourable J. Michael MacDonald, who also happens to be a native of Whitney Pier.

My appointment was also historic because I would be the first vice-regal in Nova Scotia history not to immediately reside

In 2008, Lieutenant-Governor Mayann Francis began a four-year commission as honorary lieutenant colonel of the Canadian Forces 3 Intelligence Company.

in Government House. This was certainly nothing to celebrate. When I met with the prime minister, his office was under the impression that Government House would be closed for a short period. The short period turned into three long, difficult years. During my period without an official residence I had experiences that, to my knowledge, no other lieutenant-governor in the history of this province had to deal with. If it wasn't for God, my family, close friends, and the people of Nova Scotia, I am not certain that I would have survived the first three years of my five-and-a-half-year appointment. The people of Nova Scotia, whose functions I attended and communities I visited, were my inspiration and my hope that things would get better.

And I cannot say enough about the three levels of the military. The respect they demonstrated is unsurpassed. In 2008, I began a four-year commission as honorary lieutenant colonel of 3 Intelligence Company, a line unit of the Canadian Armed Forces, an incredible and humbling experience. Another highlight and accomplishment was a trip on a training mission flight with the Royal Canadian Air Force aboard a Sea King helicopter to Sable Island. And while I was in office, the Royal Canadian Navy celebrated its 100th anniversary. In recognition of this milestone, I renamed the portico of Government House "The Gangway," with a plaque proudly displaying this honour. At the invitation of the Navy, I became the first lieutenant-governor in Nova Scotia to do an overnight voyage on a battleship, sailing on HMCS *Athabaskan* from Halifax to Cape Breton. It was both fascinating and emotional when I sailed into Sydney Harbour. Waiting for me were my family, members of the church where I worshipped as a child, and our devoted veterans.

I have a special place in my heart for our veterans. As I said to a veteran who fought for our freedoms in the Second World War, his sacrifice allowed citizens to fight for equality and justice. His fight paved the way for me to become lieutenant-governor of our beautiful province. My saddest moments were when I attended the funerals of soldiers killed in Afghanistan. Months after the funerals, I met privately with some of the families. It was heartbreaking to hear the stories of these young soldiers.

My aides-de-camp, who were RCMP, Halifax Regional Police, Army, Navy, and Air Force, all of them volunteers, gave me excellent service. I will always be grateful for their time, commitment, and the respect they showed to the office of the lieutenant-governor and to me personally as the Queen's representative. The commission-aires assigned to Government House performed their duties with class and dignity. I am also grateful for their service and dedication.

Several women volunteered their time to assist me with my wardrobe and attendance at certain events. They played the role of lady-in-waiting. Thank heavens they would arrive on time to relieve me from struggling with a zipper in the back of my dress or gown, check to make certain the lipstick was on my lips and not my teeth, that there were no runs in my pantyhose, that my hair was in place.... Ladies, you know what I am talking about. Need I continue? You get the picture. After all, I was single and needed their assistance.

MY INSTALLATION ceremony took place in the Red Room of Province House. I felt a personal sense of connection to the Red Room because of the portrait of Queen Charlotte, who is from the Black Portugese Royal House. She was the wife of King George III. Few people realize that Queen Charlotte was a Black woman. So Meghan, the Duchess of Sussex, is not the first Black person to become part of the royal family.

My family, including my brother, sister, niece, and cousin from the United States, close friends, and many members of the public were there to witness this historic ceremony. In my speech, I said,

> *The role of the lieutenant-governor is more than just ceremonial. The lieutenant-governor is intrinsically tied to the tradition of responsible government in Nova Scotia. Province House witnessed the birth of responsible government in the nineteenth century. One of my predecessors, Joseph Howe, spoke passionately in favour of responsible government and freedom of the press within these very walls. He understood the importance of the relationship between the various branches of government— executive, legislative, and judiciary.*

The office of the lieutenant-governor brings to bear moral influence. There is a will to prevent harm to our system of government and our democracy. The importance of the constitutional responsibility of the Crown was clear to me. For that reason, not being a constitutional expert and recognizing that I was taking on this responsibility during a time when Nova Scotia had a minority government, I brought together a team of people to share their knowledge and experience with me, experts in law and politics, a historian, and Dr. Peter Aucoin of Dalhousie University's School of Public Administration. This group was not there to advise me; the only advisor to a vice-regal representative is the prime minister for the governor general or the premier for the lieutenant-governor.

Mayann Francis wanted to receive a blessing from God before her installation as lieutenant-governor of Nova Scotia on Sept. 7, 2006. She arranged a service at All Saints Cathedral in Halifax; her brother-in-law, Archbishop Vincent M. Waterman, played a role in the service. (PROVINCE OF NOVA SCOTIA)

Instead I wanted them to share with me their knowledge of various scenarios I could face with a minority government in power.

We have witnessed several situations within the last ten years where the Queen's representative had to make a critical constitutional decision. In 2008 the Governor General was asked by the Prime Minister to prorogue Parliament in anticipation of a no-confidence vote on the budget. The request was granted, which has remained the subject of much debate.

After the May 2017 election in British Columbia, the Liberal party was reduced to minority status by a slim margin. The New Democratic Party (NDP) joined forces with the Green Party, which gave them a majority. Together they passed a vote of no confidence in the Liberal government. The Lieutenant-Governor rejected the Premier's advice to call a new election. Instead she invited the NDP to form the next government. Subsequently, the Premier submitted her resignation to the Lieutenant-Governor.

The 2018 election in New Brunswick is another example. When the Liberal government did not win a majority of seats, the sitting premier met with the Lieutenant-Governor and got her permission to form the government. Within months of the election the Liberal government lost the confidence of the House. The Lieutenant-Governor accepted the resignation of the Premier and subsequently asked the Opposition party to form the government.

Fortunately there were no constitutional matters like the above while I was lieutenant-governor. If there had been, I was ready, willing, and prepared to make a decision based on the constitution, precedent, and legal opinion.

One of the constitutional duties I enjoyed was the reading of the Speech from the Throne. The afternoon leading up to the speech was filled with pomp and circumstance, like wearing the Civil Uniform and performing an inspection of the guard. Some throne speeches I delivered were longer than others. Many people believe that lieutenant-governors have input into the speech. No they do not. The government in power serves at the pleasure of the Crown, and as the Crown's representative, the lieutenant-governor reads the government's agenda as prepared by the government.

Needless to say, one of the highlights of my tenure was meeting the Queen. This great honour happened twice during my time in office. All appointed lieutenant-governors and governors general meet Her Majesty. Because I was not married, I was permitted to take a close family relative. When I asked my sister if she wanted to meet the Queen, she at first thought I was joking. I should note that my sister is afraid of flying. When she realized that I was not joking, she said, "That means we have to fly across the ocean."

I said, "Yes, we cannot take the train."

On May 30, 2007, Lieutenant-Governor Mayann Francis (right) and her sister Isabel met Her Majesty Queen Elizabeth II. (COURTESY OF AUTHOR)

"Well, I can't go over all that water."

I said, "Okay."

I then called her husband and said, "This is the deal. Talk to your wife, buy her a bottle of gin or whatever, because she is coming to London to meet the Queen."

On May 30, 2007, exactly one year to the day since the Prime Minister asked me to be the vice-regal representative, Isabel and I met Her Majesty. We travelled to London with an aide-de-camp, and the three of us were booked into separate rooms at the Fleming Mayfair Hotel. Before leaving Halifax, we had received briefings by email from Ottawa. Hats and gloves were optional. We were advised that a lady-in-waiting would be at Buckingham Palace to meet us and speak to us further about the audience with the Queen and to show us when and how to curtsey. My sister and I decided to wear suits for our meeting with Her Majesty. We also wore hats and gloves and carried purses. We met with Her Majesty for close to fifteen minutes, I think. I did not time our meeting; I felt like I was dreaming.

After our audience with Her Majesty, Isabel and I looked at each other in disbelief. It was such an honour to be in the company of the Queen. Many people have asked me, "What is she like?" I found her warm, engaging, intelligent, sincere, and gracious. She is an amazing woman. When I was with her, I knew that I was standing in the presence of greatness. The conversation she had with my sister made it clear that she had done her homework on Isabel's background. I have never revealed our private conversation with the Queen, and do not intend to do so here.

Despite the challenge of not living in Government House for three years, I did my best to ensure that I fulfilled my role with class and dignity. As I said earlier, the people of Nova Scotia gave me my strength. Every time I visited a fire hall and spent time in a community, I came away with a renewed spirit and energy. This is why I created the Community Spirit Award, which I launched in Sydney on September 26, 2007, at the Celebrating Communities Conference. At the launch, I said that the award

> will acknowledge and celebrate Nova Scotia communities that work. Places where members care for each other, interact with each other, lift each other. The award is, in effect, a homage to my own home community of Whitney Pier, a place where people truly cared about each other.

The first community to receive this award was Port Morien, Cape Breton, on July 27, 2008. I was thrilled and honoured when during the award ceremony, I was made an honorary citizen of this warm and friendly community. Many rural communities received this award during my tenure. The Lieutenant-Governor Community Spirit Award is still active.

I also created the Lieutenant-Governor Hope and Inspiration Award at the Nova Scotia Community College (NSCC). Education for me is like gold, very valuable. I strongly believe that education opens many doors and can change someone's life. I am not exclusively talking about a university education, which is important. We also need community college graduates and the skilled trades. When I relocated to New York and was having difficulty finding employment with only my bachelor's degree, I drew upon my skills and training as an X-ray technician and found employment. This is one of the reasons I am very passionate about skills-based education.

My goal in creating the award was to ensure that all students had the opportunity to complete their education. So often students find themselves in financial difficulties in the middle of their program and may have to leave college. I wanted the award to help them stay in school. I also wanted the award to recognize the importance of NSCC. A skills-based education can help graduates compete in a highly technical environment, locally, nationally, and internationally. Many graduates of NSCC become entrepreneurs. This can only be good for our economy both locally and nationally.

NSCC valued the award at $1,000 and made funds available on all thirteen campuses throughout the province. When I left office I made certain the award was endowed, and now the Honourable Mayann E. Francis Hope and Inspiration Award is, through the generosity of many donors. I was surprised and humbled when NSCC also named the library on the Marconi Campus, in Sydney, Cape Breton, the Honourable Mayann E. Francis Library.

Other awards created during my tenure were:

 * Lieutenant-Governor's Faith in Action Award, Atlantic School of Theology, for people who put their faith to work by helping those in need (this award has since been named in my honour, the Honourable Mayann E. Francis Faith in Action Award);

* Lieutenant-Governor's Intergenerational Award, Mount Saint Vincent University, to recognize graduating students who volunteered their time to work with seniors and youth
* Lieutenant-Governor's Volunteerism Award, Nova Scotia; College of Art and Design (now NSCAD University), given to graduating students who demonstrate their commitment to their community by volunteering;
* Lieutenant-Governor's Persons with Disabilities Employer Partnership Award, which focuses attention on the accomplishments of persons with disabilities and employers who employ and accommodate members of this community.

Lieutenant-governors are not obliged to carry on the work of their predecessor. To my knowledge the two lieutenant-governor's awards still in existence are the Community Spirit Award and the Persons with Disabilities Employer Partnership Award.

I was deeply moved by many people and events during my tenure. One such event, to which I was invited by the Monarchist League of New Glasgow, took place in Pictou. Members of the military, veterans, RCMP, regional police officers, and a piper were there to greet me. Rose petals lined the walkway. It was a beautiful sunny day and I was overwhelmed, filled with joy. A comment made by a teenager in one of the rural communities I visited also stands out. He was asked what he thought about the lieutenant-governor. Reportedly, he said, "She smells nice." When asked what he meant, I am told he looked up at the sky, hesitated, then said, "She smells like heaven." The woman who related the story to me said she was speechless. And so was I.

There are so many beautiful stories to share I cannot possibly fit them into this memoir. Travelling the length and breadth of this province was always a pleasure and a favourite part of my tenure. I liked being with the people. This is why I made it a priority to take the office of lieutenant-governor to them, let the people see me and talk to me. I wanted to demystify the office. Spending time with seniors, youth, faith leaders, and veterans filled me with pride and peace. Meeting such a diversity of people enriched me as I travelled around the province from the Prestons, to the Pubnicos, to Meat Cove. It truly was a blessing to be the Queen's representative and to have this opportunity to serve Nova Scotians. Bestowing awards on deserving Nova Scotians who have helped make our province strong was such an honour. I learned from the public. The public helped me grow into my role as the Queen's representative.

When I met world leaders, I always had to pinch myself, the Black girl from Whitney Pier, now a woman greeting powerful and influential people. It was such a privilege. Among them were Queen Sophia of Spain, Condoleezza Rice, who was Secretary of State under President George W. Bush, David Dodge, former governor of the Bank of Canada, the Governor General of Antigua and Barbuda, the prime minister of Antigua and Barbuda, the prime minister and Governor General of St. Kitts, the Grand Master of the Order of Malta, as well as influential entertainers, artists, and many more.

One meeting I must share with you was when the Cuban ambassador made a courtesy call to my office at the Maritime Centre. Toward the end of our meeting, I told him my dad was Cuban. Well, he lost his diplomatic posture and jumped from his seat with excitement, claiming me as their own. A Cuban friend of mine who heard him speak later in the day said he proudly boasted about the Cuban lieutenant-governor.

Chapter 9

"AN OFFICIAL HOMELESS SITUATION"

*I look to the mountains; where will my help come from?
My help will come from the Lord, who made heaven and
earth.*

PSALM 121:1

My friend the Honourable Wayne Adams had a regular column with the now defunct *Daily News*. Wayne Adams was the first African Nova Scotian member of the legislative assembly and cabinet minister. When he was minister of the environment, he introduced the solid-waste management strategy, considered the most comprehensive in Canada. As a result, Nova Scotia became a world leader in the field of recycling. He also introduced the Wilderness Areas Protection Act and Canada's first fully integrated emergency 911 system. He is recipient of the Order of Canada, the Order of Nova Scotia (conferred by me in 2011), the Harry Jerome Award, and many other prestigious awards. In his column on September 12, 2007, under the title "Francis Brings Elegance, Substance to New Role," he wrote, "There is no personal joy on my part to see our first Black lieutenant-governor in an official homeless situation, so like her, I beseech the Province and its public works department to have Her Honour in her appropriate address real soon."

There were rumours that some people in government, both on the political and the bureaucratic side, did not want me to ever reside in Government House. Was it that they did not support or believe in the monarchy? Or was it because I am Black? A credible source told me that a high-level member of the provincial legislature stated: "If I had my way, she would not get in that house." The credible source added that a white businessman remarked to them that some contractors had an aversion to working on Government House just for a Black woman to move in. There was speculation that Government House could have been available for a new lieutenant-governor sooner than it was. A well-known, respected religious leader, who was upset about my situation, asked if there was anything they could do to help, adding that if Premier Hamm were in power he would have made sure that everything was done to speed up the completion of the renovations.

Something a senior bureaucrat said to me when I complained about renovations taking too long and I explained that it was increasingly difficult to live in my condo was proof to me that members of the government and bureaucracy were not prepared for or pleased about an historic and different appointment. They said, "No one expected the lieutenant-governor would be someone living in a condo. Everyone thought it would be someone from the south end or Bridgewater." In other words, they were not expecting that someone from humble beginnings, someone Black, would be the prime minister's choice. There did not appear to be a commitment to make certain that I would not remain, as Wayne Adams noted, "in an official homeless situation."

Another senior bureaucrat with years of experience in the public service, someone I respected for their intelligence and honesty, once said in passing that if the government wanted the renovations on Government House to be completed, they need only give the word. I do not know where the truth lies. What I do know is the psychological pain and humiliation I endured. The disrespect demonstrated by some members of the legislature and government officials at times left me speechless and distraught. Writing this memoir has resurrected painful memories, not only about not being a resident of Government House for most of my tenure, but also about being forced to justify anything I requested. I buried my pain because I was committed to the call to serve, regardless of what I was experiencing.

I will always be grateful to the many supporters who quietly lobbied the Premier with letters and phone calls, or spoke to him at functions, voicing their disgust about the length of time it was taking to complete the renovations on Government House and often questioning why the government did not immediately find an official residence suitable for the Queen's representative and staff. They also complained about what seemed like intermittent work being done on Government House prior to 2009. I still meet people who ask if I had the opportunity to live in Government House. When I tell them yes, they always express relief and happiness.

Staff and I managed to keep the office going for the three years that we were out of Government House. Not having an official residence was stressful for me and not easy for them either. Among other things, it was their job to find appropriate venues for functions. While Province House was a venue we could use, it was only available to us when the House was not sitting or the space was not in use by elected officials. An official residence, whether Government

House or another similar residence sufficient to accommodate staff and hold functions, would have eliminated some of the challenges staff faced and relieved the pressure that I was experiencing. Three years seemed like an eternity. In many ways it was.

The Rodney MacDonald government was defeated in June 2009. With their defeat, I was certain that my chances were good for moving into Government House before the scheduled end of my tenure in September 2011. The election of an NDP government gave hope that something would be done about yet another negative distinction having been added to Nova Scotia's record of racial intolerance and indifference, with the first Black lieutenant-governor not having the privilege of residing in Government House, the official vice-regal residence.

The confidence I placed in the NDP government had nothing to do with partisan politics. It had everything to do with my "gut instinct." The lieutenant-governor should and must be above partisan politics. As Lincoln Alexander said in his memoir, *Go to School, You're a Little Black Boy*, "The lieutenant-governor performs functions similar to those of the monarch and is beyond partisan politics." When I was appointed as the Queen's representative, many people believed that I was in some way connected to the Prime Minister. I most certainly was not! When I was a public servant, I always kept my politics private because I believed my role was to implement policy regardless of the government in power. Just to be clear, I met Mr. Harper for the first time on May 30, 2006, when he asked me to be the thirty-first lieutenant-governor of Nova Scotia.

My optimism to one day live in Government House under an NDP government was influenced by a series of events that took place under the previous government from the time Ottawa announced in June 2006 that I would be the next lieutenant-governor. Based on my conversations with Ottawa, I do not believe they knew the full extent of the renovations the government was planning for Government House. When I was installed in September 2006, the renovations were scheduled to be completed by December 2008. Subsequently that was changed to 2009. An entry in one of my journals mentions another anticipated completion date of March 2010.

There was speculation that a royal visit might be made to Nova Scotia in 2010. I was told by a reliable source that a member of the legislature indicated that it would not be appropriate for the lieutenant-governor to move into Government House prior to a royal visit. If that statement is true, and I have no reason to doubt what was told to me, it should be clear why my hope of moving into Government House came alive with the election of a new government.

Believing that renovations would be completed by 2008, in my installation speech I said:

> *How appropriate that Government House will reopen in December of 2008 as a symbol of renewal and rebirth during the celebration of another birth—Christmas. I will remain in my own private residence in Halifax. I am sure you would agree that this is a more feasible and cost effective arrangement. It avoids the added cost and disruption of having to move twice and allows for me to effectively discharge my duties and responsibilities as lieutenant-governor. While this interim arrangement is a first for Nova Scotia—and, I hope, the last time it is necessary—I am committed to ensuring that the status and dignity afforded to the role of lieutenant-governor is maintained during this period. I am confident that the work to restore Government House will be completed on time for reopening in December 2008. It would be unfortunate for a lieutenant-governor not to be able to take [up] residence at Government House during their tenure, and I know the government and I would prefer that this not be part of my legacy.*

I believed the government was sincere. I had no reason to suspect that they were not.

It has been over fifty years since the Black residents of Africville were torn from their community. Nova Scotia will always be haunted by how the people of Africville were treated. Oh yes, an apology was issued and a museum erected, and a road bearing the name Africville is recognition that an injustice based on race was done. To this day there are people who honestly believe that the City did the community a favour because they were living in squalor. The question is, why were they living in squalor? In his book *Viola Desmond's Canada*, Dr. Graham Reynolds gives an insight into a possible answer: "Through isolation, neglect, and prejudice, Africville underwent a process of ghettoization, and the residents were left to fend for themselves without many of the basic essentials such as running water and police service."

If I did not live in Government House, I believe—like the debates and discussions around Viola Desmond, Africville, and the unresolved African Nova Scotian land claims—it would be a challenge for the government of the day to explain why. It would have been another negative mark on the history of race relations in Nova Scotia.

When a lieutenant-governor resides in Government House, many activities take place in-house. The lieutenant-governor's fully equipped office is located there. Offices for staff are also located on-site. And of course, there are the private quarters for the lieutenant-governor. When there is a function in the House, the lieutenant-governor is escorted from the quarters to whatever room the function is taking place in. This arrangement certainly makes life easier for the lieutenant-governor. Everything is in place to support the role. The chef is there to attend to the dietary needs of the lieutenant-governor and guests. Housekeepers are on-site for Government House and for the lieutenant-governor's private quarters. The driver takes the lieutenant-governor to events outside of Government House. If, for example, for one week all events are on-site, the driver's hours are greatly reduced, compared to a vice-regal who resides outside of Government House and must be transported on a daily basis to and from an office and to events around the city or province. The convenience of residing in Government House cannot be overstated.

In Ontario there is no vice-regal residence; however, the lieutenant-governor has a suite of offices in Queen's Park. Lincoln Alexander describes the suite in his memoir:

> *The grandeur of the lieutenant-governor's suite is not lost on those who visit it. Its deep red carpeting projected a regal feel for anyone who entered the two-storey vice-regal suite. The high ceilings and rich oak paneling infused the setting with a noble atmosphere where one would expect affairs of state to be carried on. The suite also boasted a library and formal reception rooms.*

When I lived in Toronto, I was fortunate to attend several functions in the lieutenant-governor's suite. It truly is a magnificent venue, very fitting for the Queen's representative.

The executive assistant to the lieutenant-governor researched other vice-regal residences across Canada, compared the results with my living arrangements, and submitted her findings to the government. The letter dated April 2, 2008, which outlined living arrangements in the nine other Canadian provinces, concluded with this statement: "As you can see, the standard for accommodations and services for the lieutenant-governor of Nova Scotia is far below the existing standard for lieutenant-governors across this country."

That statement said it all. Whether consciously or unconsciously, the government, in my opinion, lowered the standard for how and where the vice-regal representative would live when the first Black lieutenant-governor was appointed. Was it incompetence? Did they not care? Was it not a priority, therefore no money was allocated to fix this injustice? Or was it differential treatment based on race and gender?

For the first three years of her tenure, the lieutenant-governor's office was in the Maritime Centre. To access the elevator from the parking garage, Mayann Francis had to walk past a garbage dumpster every day. (COURTESY OF AUTHOR)

For the first three years of my tenure, the office for the lieutenant-governor was in the Maritime Centre, a public office building with no private access for the Queen's representative or visiting dignitaries. Some dignitaries and members of the royal family did not pay the customary official courtesy call to our office because of privacy and security concerns. When Prince Andrew was in Halifax, our private meeting took place at Stadacona, a secure military venue. He did not hold back on his views about my not having an official residence in which to live or to host visiting dignitaries!

The lieutenant-governor's vehicle was parked underground. To access the elevator from the parking garage, I had to walk daily by the garbage dumpster to the public elevator. Because of where the Maritime Centre is located, there was no place for the vehicle to park in front of the building. When aides-de-camp came to perform their duties, there was no reserved parking for their vehicle.

Maritime Centre is located just up the street from Government House, on the same block. Interestingly, my office overlooked Government House. So I watched with a heavy heart how slowly the renovations were proceeding. There were days when it appeared that no work was being done. I first thought this was my imagination until members of the public began to make the same observations.

For the inconvenience of not having the privileges and advantages of other lieutenant-governors, I was given an allowance. I quote from a letter I received from the government, dated October 4, 2006.

> *An arrangement was made for you to remain in your personal condominium and receive an allowance of $6,000 per month. The funds are to cover costs associated with meal preparation, domestic services, home security, heating, and electricity. Also, these funds are being provided to you for receptions and functions within your condominium and as it relates to your position as lieutenant-governor.*

There was public outrage at this allotment. I certainly understood the anger. There are those who do not support the monarchy, and others believed it was a waste of money to pay me to live in my condo.

When I spoke with Lincoln Alexander, he expressed his outrage at how long it was taking the government to complete the renovations on Government House. He asked if the government was compensating me for the inconvenience of not having the privileges available to me that previous lieutenant-governors had. When I told him the amount of my allowance, he was appalled and was further angered when I said I was living in my condo until the renovations were completed. He told me that I should invite him to Nova Scotia. I did not invite him to Halifax. I am sure if I did his presence would not have gone unnoticed. In retrospect I wish I had invited him.

I'm not certain what he had in mind, but I am sure he would have voiced his concern about my living and working conditions. I will never know.

Speaking with Lincoln Alexander gave me the boost I so badly needed. An entry in my journal said my talk with him came at the right time. I also wrote in my journal that I had been a fool to accept this arrangement. I now believe the government knew the house would not be ready by 2008. It was due to my ignorance about the detail and privileges of the role and my trust in the government that I accepted this living arrangement. I was not prepared for the anxiety and stress of not having an official residence.

Before our offices in the Maritime Centre were ready, we worked out of Province House. Even though the Maritime Centre was not an ideal location, staff stood firm in making certain that the design of the temporary offices would allow the lieutenant-governor to carry out the duties of a vice-regal representative with dignity. When it was time to relocate, office staff told me that they needed to find a desk for me. The desk I was using, which we had been told we could take with us on loan, was no longer offered because it belonged to the premier's inventory. An email suggested that staff "buy a desk off the floor at Office Interiors or a similar business." Word quickly spread that the lieutenant-governor did not have a desk. A bureaucrat I had previously worked with was angered by the news and found a suitable desk.

I needed a computer for my home, but the request was denied. You see, in an official residence like Government House, a computer would not be needed in the private quarters because the lieutenant-governor would simply go to their office downstairs. When I informed a senior official that my family and I would purchase one for my home office, suddenly the request was granted. The person who was charged to purchase the computer was extremely thorough, respectful, and professional.

At the annual Conference of Lieutenant-Governors and Territorial Commissioners of Canada, held in Regina, Saskatchewan, in April 2007, Dr. Michael Jackson, CVO, CD, presented his paper on "The Crown in Today's Federal State." In it he said he believed "vice-regal people should indeed use their prestigious offices for strengthening civil society." He was impressed by lieutenant-governors who became active in worthy causes. He viewed this as a new trend. He quoted from three installation speeches made by new lieutenant-governors that he felt demonstrated this trend. I was one of those lieutenant-governors. His reference was about my commitment to community: "The Honourable Mayann Francis of Nova Scotia spoke at her installation of 'a central vision of what it means to be a healthy and strong community.'"

My desire to focus on community during my tenure meant that I would travel extensively throughout the province. I believed it was important for me as the Queen's representative to get out and be with the people of this province. On one occasion while travelling to an event, the driver mistakenly made a wrong turn, which caused me to be over thirty-five minutes late. It is important for lieutenant-governors to arrive on time for functions. There is a tremendous amount of work on the part of the staff, aides-de-camp, and organizers to ensure that protocols are in order. Timing is critical to the smooth functioning of events. To make matters worse, there was no way to contact the organizers because there was no cellphone tower in this rural part of the province, and the driver's cellphone would not work. Our late arrival was very embarrassing and impacted negatively on the Office. The organizers, dignitaries, and guests were gracious. They were glad we had arrived safely.

As a result of this incident we requested a GPS system for our assigned vehicle, an older model car that did not have a built-in system. Our request was denied. An email to our office dated October 10, 2007, said,

The L.G. vehicle is slated for replacement next fiscal year. Most, if not all, luxury vehicles of late vintage have a GPS or equivalent system as standard equipment so as to help one to navigate the highways and byways of this fair province. Thus a GPS stand-alone unit would be inappropriate at this time. Cellphones will assist in the event of difficulty (being lost, for example).

For the safety of the driver, the aide-de-camp, and me, and for the dignity and respect of the office, I was prepared to purchase a GPS unit with my personal money. Fortunately, I did not have to. The staff placed the credibility of the office as top priority and purchased a GPS unit from discretionary funds until a new car was purchased. After we purchased the unit, staff received this email, dated October 22, 2007: "If your office in the meantime has acquired a hand-held GPS unit, please be advised that the cost of same will reduce whatever funding remains yet in place for other priorities. Also I assume that there would be no need to have a replacement vehicle with a built-in system."

Apparently, prior to 2006, new lieutenant-governors were given the option of the purchase of a new vehicle. I was never made aware of this. I was not interested in a purchase of a new vehicle so early in my tenure. In my opinion, the vehicle I inherited was still working well. The question is, why wasn't I given the option, if this was the standard practice at that time? Or did this practice stop as soon as it was announced that I would be lieutenant-governor?

The use of the car and the driver's hours necessarily increased substantially during the three years I lived in my condo. The wear and tear on the vehicle soon became evident. In 2007, invoices for car repairs totalled over $6,000, not including routine checks. In a letter to the authorities responsible for the oversight of the car, dated September 4, 2007, staff pointed out concerns about the starter, cruise control, air conditioner, electrical issues, and tire rim seals. The email's author said: "Her Honour's road trips are extensive and this will continue for the duration of her term." The author also mentioned concern for the health and safety of the lieutenant-governor and her driver.

> *Her Honour's official car is well over six years old, has travelled over 174,000 km. Given all of the aforementioned information and the fact that previous lieutenant-governors were provided with a new official car, or at least given the option of a new vehicle following their installation, I believe it is time to review this matter and look into the option of a new vehicle for the lieutenant-governor's use before a serious situation occurs.*

Here is the email, dated September 13, 2007, that staff received in response: "A safe vehicle is imperative and we will not put the LG at risk of harm. A new vehicle is not budgeted in this year and may be something that could be looked at next year. I will bring this to the attention of...."

The wear and tear on the car and my increased travel led to the suggestion that I was using the car inappropriately, that I did not always use the car for official business. I certainly admit to being driven to doctor appointments, church, and on the rare occasion to stores. None of my family members ever utilized the car. When I took vacation, I was driven to the airport to catch a plane; I was never driven to a holiday location within Nova Scotia. I did not go on leisurely drives around the province.

The Office responded to the personal use of the vehicle and the driver's increased hours in another letter to the governing authority with the same date as the letter mentioned above, September 4, 2007. In part the letter said this:

> *Her Honour has a disability that affects her eyesight, and there is a duty to accommodate. This affects the driver's hours in two ways. First, this disability prevents Her Honour from driving,*

and she must depend on the chauffeur to transport her where she needs to go. Second, this disability is a safety concern when Her Honour is out in public. Her Honour's peripheral vision is affected and therefore she is unable to see people approaching her from the side. This makes it necessary for the driver to accompany Her Honour when she is out in public and not assisted by an aide-de-camp.

There is absolutely no doubt that the driver's hours increased 100 percent when I took office, as stated in a memo to the governing authority dated April 2, 2008, regarding the impact of the closure of Government House. Without an official residence, it was not uncommon for me to be in and out of the vehicle up to five or more times a day, especially if there were more than three functions not held at the Maritime Centre. For each event there was usually a change of clothing, which meant that I had to be transported back to my residence to change. If there was a change in aide-de-camp (ADC), the driver would transport them back to their vehicle, then pick up the newly assigned ADC. Without an official residence, there was no place for the ADCs to park their cars. This back and forth by the driver certainly increased his hours. This meant that the driver's current contract had to be renegotiated with the union. And rightly so.

My office presented a chart to the government to demonstrate that the driver and the vehicle were not being abused. This chart compared vehicle usage for the driver when Government House was open and after Government House closed in September 2006. Some of the staff had worked in the office for over a decade, and they were aware of past practices. In addition, the driver had logged his travels with lieutenant-governors dating back decades. It was clear from the chart that I did not take unnecessary advantage of the driver, and the suggestion that I had used the vehicle improperly was put to rest. I think there was no desire to open a conversation about past use of the vehicle for unofficial business. The chart clearly showed that compared to past practices, my use of the vehicle was dictated by my current circumstances, not by abuse.

John Morrison, my driver at the time, eventually received a new negotiated contract, and there were backup drivers to cover weekends and holidays. He deserved a new contract. His loyalty to the office is to be commended. And I thank him for his service to me as lieutenant-governor.

Discussions in the office about the need for a new vehicle intensified when it became clear to the drivers that the current vehicle was unpredictable and, in their view, no longer safe. In August 2008, the coordinator of the three support drivers outlined his concerns in a letter to me. It should be noted that the coordinator was once the primary VIP limo driver for a prime minister's vehicle and was an RCMP VIP driver until his retirement. His letter focused once again on safety. He wrote,

> We have little confidence in this car. Although it is well maintained, wear and tear has become more pronounced. We just don't know what will go wrong next, and more importantly, when. Keeping it presentable is challenging and keeping it mechanically sound is expensive and unreliable. If I was a taxi driver, the current limo would make a great taxi, but you should not be chauffeured in a taxi.

To further support the need for a new vehicle, in February 2008 the coordinator produced a research report titled *Replacement Limousine Research for Lieutenant-Governor of Nova Scotia*, dated February 12, 2008. The information contained in this detailed report and his letter to me were shared with the government officials.

I cannot overemphasize the commitment of the staff and the drivers and their determination to win this unnecessary and time-consuming battle. When permission was finally granted for a replacement vehicle, we were faced with another barrier.

By this time I was tired. I wrote in my journal, "I try not to think about how I am being treated because it only makes me angry, then I become depressed." My whole life is about climbing over barriers. My foundation and strength to keep fighting come from God. I was determined that the barriers would never break my spirit.

When several vehicles that clearly were not suited for vice-regal purposes were recommended (including a hybrid SUV), the office had to fight for something more appropriate. Office staff made contact with lieutenant-governors across the country regarding their vehicles, and this information outlined the advantages and disadvantages of a hybrid SUV. At my request the coordinator of the backup drivers evaluated the government's recommended vehicles. I shared his evaluation of the vehicles in a letter I wrote to the governing authority dated September 23, 2008. What follows is part of the coordinator's feedback to me.

> *The LG vehicle selection must be considered "outside the box" when compared to standard government vehicle issue. The smaller cars just can't meet the physical and administrative needs of the Office. You are not just selecting a vehicle for a driver—it must be for the rear passenger first (30,000 km per year in the back seat is a long time, and comfort cannot be compromised). None of the suggested alternatives have the work space in the front or back. (Front Bench Seats as outlined in "Report" and listed as a spec.) When the report specs are met, the so-called green cars don't make the grade.*

The office was finally successful in this battle. And thank heavens we were. At the request of the Queen's security detail, the Lincoln Town Car Signature L was used for Her Majesty during her 2010 visit.

My staff fully supported me in the vehicle fight. I am sure at times they felt frustrated because every step of the way for three years, I had been fighting battles that I am sure previous lieutenant-governors never had to face. Staff had to defend and fight for what was needed and appropriate for the Queen's representative. I commend staff for standing up for what they knew was just and fair.

I recall very early in my tenure my request for a communications person to write speeches. Vice-regal representatives usually hit the ground running, so from my perspective a speechwriter is of utmost importance. If I'd had the luxury of time I would have written my own speeches to address the immediate need. I was offered someone whom I rejected, to the anger of a couple of people. I rejected the person not because the person did not have great credentials but because in my observation the person's political ties were very apparent. The vice-regal office must be above politics and not be perceived as partisan; as I said in my installation speech, "It must never be compromised either by partisan appearance or actions."

A senior bureaucrat sent an email to staff in response to my request for a meeting to further discuss communication needs. Staff immediately brought the email to my attention. After I read it, I shook my head, not in disbelief but in disappointment at the tone of the letter. I was taken by surprise; I always held this person in high regard. Many Black people believe that no matter how high we climb, we will experience micro-aggression, a term coined by psychiatrist Chester M. Pierce, "a subtle but offensive comment or action directed at a minority or other non-dominant group that is often unintentional or unconsciously reinforces a stereotype." I could not help but ask myself, would this person have responded in the same manner if I had been white?

When President Obama delivered his first congressional speech, a member of the congress shouted, "You lie." This was the first time in the history of the United States that such an outburst of disrespect was demonstrated toward a president during a congressional speech. Would this have happened if the president were white? Something was triggered in the subconscious mind of the people in my case and Obama's case that permitted them to lower the standard of respect. It did not matter if he was the president of the United States, the most powerful office in the free world, and it did not matter if I was the lieutenant-governor of Nova Scotia, the highest ranking person in the province. The standard for respect in both instances was lowered. (I received a written apology from the bureaucrat. President Obama also received an apology.)

Micro-aggression was also evident when people who knew better refused to follow protocol and address me in public situations as "Your Honour." Fortunately the majority of people did follow protocol, and for this I am grateful.

Putting this memoir together has been for me a roller coaster of emotions. At times I wanted to give in and let the project go because I found many aspects of my research, including the review of my journals, very painful. For example, I wrote in my journal about something distressing that happened to me in the House of Assembly one morning during my tenure: "March 25, 2010, 11 A.M. I prorogued the House this morning. When I walked into the chamber a deliberate, loud sigh came from the _____ party front bench. How disgusting and disrespectful." (In my journal, I name the party.)

When this happened, I could not help but think about allegations made by Nova Scotia's only Black MLA in 2007. In "On the Cusp of Change?: The Nova Scotia House of Assembly," a 2008 study published in the *Canadian Parliamentary Review*, the authors, Jennifer Smith and Lori Turnbull, report that Percy Paris alleged he was subjected to "subtle and persistent" racism in the legislature. Meanwhile his colleague, who is Indo-Canadian, indicated he did not experience what Percy experienced; instead, he experienced rudeness.

Was the individual's sigh that morning in March a gesture of childish, rude behaviour, disrespect for the vice-regal office and the legislature? Was it because I was Black and did not deserve respect? Or was the person just tired and did not mean to let out a sigh loud enough for me to hear? As I took my place at the Speaker's chair I glanced at the party in question. It was like looking at a group of elementary schoolchildren who were trying to hide what they just did because they knew it was wrong. I hid my disappointment and the pain I was feeling and proceeded to perform my constitutional duty with dignity. As Michelle Obama, former first lady of the United States said, "When they go low, you go high." I agree. And I say, when they go in the gutter, you step onto the curb.

WHEN CANADIANS woke up on June 10, 2009, they did so to the news that the NDP would be forming a majority government in Nova Scotia for the first time in the province's history. Following a provincial general election, the constitutional duties of the lieutenant-governor come immediately into play. In this situation there was a clear majority. Subsequently, the outgoing premier would tender his resignation to me. Legally, he would remain premier until the new premier was sworn in. After Premier MacDonald tendered his resignation, I asked Darrell Dexter, leader of the NDP, to assume the office of premier and president of the executive council.

The historic swearing-in ceremony of the first NDP government in Nova Scotia took place on June 19, 2009, at the Cunard Centre. I remember that day as though it were yesterday. I felt honoured to play a role in our democratic process. It was an emotional moment as well, because a little Black girl from Whitney Pier was continuing to make history. I could not help but think about my parents.

At our first meeting after the swearing-in, Premier Dexter made a commitment to me that I would take up residence in Government House in December of that year, six months hence. He was serious and sincere. When our meeting ended, I did not know whether to shout for joy or cry. For the first time in three years, I knew I was definitely going to reside in Government House before the end of my tenure. Someone in a position of authority finally cared.

Darryl Dexter kept his word.

Chapter 10

THE BIG MOVE

And the God of all grace, who called you to His eternal glory in Christ, after you have suffered a little while, will Himself restore you and make you strong, firm, and steadfast.

1 PETER 5:10

In a few weeks, on December 11, 2009, I would be moving to live in Government House, the thirty-first lieutenant-governor to do so. The first was Sir John Wentworth, who had ordered the government of the day to build a suitable residence for the person appointed to the vice-regal office. The cornerstone to the Georgian mansion was laid in 1800, and Wentworth and his wife moved in five years later.

As much as I loved my condo, I was no longer happy living there as lieutenant-governor. It soon became an overcrowded burden. In order to accommodate the additional clothing—hats, shoes, garments—a large clothing rack had to be purchased, which made my bedroom look like a factory outlet with windows.

Cooked food delivered by the people who were hired to prepare my meals or to be picked up and delivered by the driver added another burden to scheduling. I had to clean and clear out my fridge to make room for weekly deliveries and clean the used containers to be returned to the caterers. Somehow, I managed to do these chores. When I performed my duties from the Maritime Centre, I took my lunch to work. For three years, I took a doggy bag to the office, probably the first lieutenant-governor to do so.

One time, I arrived back at my condo from an event late into the evening. Tired and hungry, I decided to have pita bread. I put it into my toaster oven then went to my bedroom. I was gone for a few seconds, only to return to find the oven in flames. The alarm went off. I panicked and foolishly threw water on the oven. Only by the grace of God I am still here after making such a stupid decision. I have never seen so much smoke in my life. When the security people called I told them that the fire department was not needed. My beloved cat Angel was traumatized. I was frustrated, tired, and angry. I could not help but think that if I had been living in Government House or if a temporary and appropriate official residence had been secured, things would have been different. There would have been a light snack prepared earlier by the chef for when I returned.

When I finally moved into Government House in December 2009, I buried deep in the recesses of my mind my three years of negative experiences. I hid my feelings because I loved being lieutenant-governor. My role as the highest ranking person in the province placed me in a position of privilege to do service for the people of Nova Scotia. I wanted to make a difference. Whether I was living in Government House or not, I was the Queen's representative and I was there to serve and to carry out my duties with honour and dignity, regardless of my circumstances.

Before I made the transition to the mansion, I had Government House blessed. In the early morning hours of December 3, 2009, I had a private blessing with a Mi'kmaw chief. He conducted a release and purification ceremony. Together we walked the entire house. The next morning, an interfaith service included Mi'kmaw smudging and drumming. The entire house and the property on which the house stood were blessed. To this private blessing I invited the Honourable Graydon Nicholas, CM, ONB, the first Aboriginal person to serve as lieutenant-governor in New Brunswick, a role he held from 2009 to 2014. I admired his deeply held spiritual views.

On December 10, there was a flag raising ceremony in front of Government House. The vice-regal flag was raised for the first time at Government House since its closure in 2006; the flag is only flown when the governor is in residence. The ceremony was arranged with the Royal Canadian Navy. It was a moment of pride for me. The sailors stood at attention. After the whistle was blown, there was a moment of silence. Then slowly the vice-regal flag was raised, followed by the Canadian flag and the flag of Nova Scotia. It was a beautiful and moving moment.

After the ceremony, I went straight into my office. I did not expect to be overwhelmed, but I was and I cried. They were tears of joy. After I composed myself, I went into the drawing room where members of the navy, including Rear Admiral Madison, were waiting along with Bill Estabrooks, Minister of Transportation. Minister Estabrooks was Acting Premier at the ceremony because Premier Dexter was away. I apologized to the minister and the admiral for my red eyes and for being emotional. When Minister Estabrooks was ready to depart, he asked if he could have a private conversation with me. In my office, he told me never to apologize for being emotional; I deserved to be in the House. He said, "God bless you."

Later that morning, one of my staff came with me to my condo to help get things ready for the movers who would be coming the next day. I thanked God knowing that I was finally going to live in Government House. I loved my condo. It simply was not a residence for the duties and protocols of the Queen's representative. When the limo arrived at the front door of Government House on December 11 and the doors opened, I walked into my new home where I would live for the next couple of years. The staff were lined up to greet me. "Welcome home," they said. It was now official. History will record me as the first Black lieutenant-governor to reside in the vice-regal home. God answered my prayers.

Setting up Government House after its long closure was not easy. Nonetheless, led by the private secretary, Dr. Christopher McCreery, MVO, staff worked to ensure that Government House ran smoothly. I am grateful for their dedication. I had lobbied for and was successful in establishing a private secretary and communications officer dedicated to the Office. There hadn't been a private secretary to the lieutenant-governor in Nova Scotia since 1939. The role is responsible for supporting the lieutenant-governor in their constitutional and ceremonial role, as well as managing Government House and its staff.

After hiding under the bed for one night, Angel finally decided to make the private quarters on the third floor her home. I did not allow her beyond the private quarters. She became known as the vice-regal cat.

As thrilled as I was to finally be living in this grand, historic home, it was not as well-appointed as one might expect. I was disappointed with the kitchen in the private quarters. I had hoped to have the opportunity to cook my own meals on weekends when I did not have events. There was a hotplate, a bar refrigerator like one you would find in a hotel room, and a microwave—no oven, even though the kitchen was large enough to accommodate full-sized appliances. I was told to use the chef's commercial kitchen on the lower level if I wanted to cook. This was not only impractical; in my view it was dangerous. I would go to the commercial kitchen, bring my food to the private quarters, and heat it in the microwave. If there had been a full refrigerator in the private quarters there would have been no need to travel to the commercial kitchen. The chef would have been able to place food in the private quarters' fridge, and all I would need to do was heat it on a full-size stove. Interestingly, after my tenure ended in April 2012, a full stove and refrigerator were placed in the private quarters. A dishwasher was added in 2017.

After I left office and when I was ready to write my story, I asked Premier Dexter why he was determined that I take up residence in Government House. He told me that immediately after he was sworn in as premier, he went on a tour of Government House. He wanted to see for himself the current state of the renovations. After that tour he made it clear to the people responsible for the renovations and those departments who had oversight over the budget and other responsibilities for the vice-regal residence that he wanted Government House completed and ready for my occupancy for December 2009. He said he did not receive any pushback; he meant business. In his view, December 2009 was non-negotiable. He had observed my performance throughout my first three years and noted that I was dedicated to the office and doing a great service and that I upheld the dignity of the role by my conduct. Premier Dexter also talked about his respect for the monarchy; he felt it was an important symbol of our democracy. His respect for the Queen can be traced back to his father, who served in the Second World War. While in London, his dad saw the role of the monarchy and developed a great respect for the royal office. This respect was passed on to his son. Premier Dexter also realized that history would harshly judge the government under whose watch the first Black lieutenant-governor did not live in Government House, the very symbol of our democracy. He did not want this legacy for his government or for our province.

This was all music to my ears. He was sincere and wise. I believe Mr. Dexter recognized and understood the perception held by many people that I was a product of differential treatment. And people's perception becomes their reality. As I previously mentioned, a high-ranking government official had said that if the government wants something done, it will happen. Premier Dexter and his government proved this statement to be true.

Premier Dexter also reverted back to the proper protocol regarding the Speech from the Throne. The Speech from the Throne is written by the government and outlines in broad terms the government's programs. Under our parliamentary system, the Queen is the head of state, and the Crown entrusts the elected government with the power to govern. As such, the government is Her Majesty's government. The Speech from the Throne, delivered by the Queen's representative (either the lieutenant-governor or the governor general), denotes this with references to "my government." In November 2007 when I read for the first time the MacDonald government's Speech from the Throne, the language was changed from "my government" to "our government." My question is, why did the MacDonald government change the language? In May and June 2006, the MacDonald government's throne speeches, read by my predecessor, referenced "my government." Their action was clearly a departure from our parliamentary system of proper protocol for the Queen and Her representative.

Two significant events that occurred under the NDP government, both in 2010, positively affected my tenure. The first was Her Majesty's visit to Nova Scotia, and the second was the granting of the Free Pardon to Viola Desmond.

I could not believe that I would have the honour of meeting Her Majesty a second time. Standing at the top of the driveway to Government House on June 28, 2010, to welcome the royal couple was another defining moment for me. Her Majesty the Queen and His Royal Highness, the Duke of Edinburgh stayed at Government House for two and a half days. Lieutenant-governors move out of Government House whenever Her Majesty visits; I stayed at the Prince George Hotel.

Because Government House had been closed for three years, Her Majesty rededicated Government House as the oldest official residence in Canada and unveiled a new plaque. I am proud to have played a role in ensuring the plaque was in four languages: English, French, Mi'kmaq, and Gaelic. I also presented Her Majesty with the ceremonial Royal Key to Government House. Subsequently, when my term ended, I suggested that the Royal Key be part of the installation ceremony for all future incoming lieutenant-governors. The outgoing lieutenant-governor would present the Royal Key to incoming lieutenant-governors as a symbol of the transfer of responsibility for Government House. This practice is now an integral part of the installation ceremonies for lieutenant-governors.

I attended a luncheon in Halifax hosted by the Prime Minister for Her Majesty. I was touched when she asked me about the book I had commissioned to be written for grade three students, *Angel and the Lieutenant-Governor,* as an early lesson in civics. It was based on a website we had created, which included a children's game called "Angel's Adventure," with my cat Angel as the title character. The goal was to educate children on the role of the lieutenant-governor in our parliamentary system. I was surprised at Her Majesty's inquiry because the book was still in draft form then. It has now been translated into three languages, French, Gaelic, and Mi'kmaq. A picture book, it tells the story of our parliamentary system and denotes historical Nova Scotian people and events.

On Her Majesty's last day in Halifax, she planted an English oak tree in the garden of Government House. As we walked together up the driveway of Government House to her vehicle, with Prince Philip behind us, we had a very nice conversation that I will always cherish. Her Majesty is truly a remarkable, wonderful person. I am grateful to have met her.

Race relations became front and centre locally and nationally when the premier, on the recommendation of Executive Council and the Attorney General, requested that I grant Viola Desmond a pardon.

Viola Desmond was a successful Black businesswoman. On November 8, 1946, she left her Halifax home in her vehicle bound for Sydney, where she wanted to expand her business. Unfortunately her car developed mechanical trouble. She stopped in New Glasgow to take her vehicle to a mechanic. What happened subsequently to Ms. Desmond shone a light on racism and racial segregation in this province and our country. Viola did not make it to Sydney. Below are excerpts from various speeches I delivered about Viola's Free Pardon.

> Since her car would take several hours to be repaired, she decided to go to the movies. And because she sat in the whites-only section in the Roseland Theatre, she was arrested and thrown into jail. It cost more to sit in the white section, but the clerk would not accept her money to pay the difference in price. Subsequently, she was convicted of tax evasion of one cent.

At a ceremony in Province House on April 15, 2010, I executed the Royal Prerogative of Mercy to grant posthumously a Free Pardon to Viola Desmond, saying,

> [it] represents the unwavering recognition of her innocence and wrongful conviction all those years before and rights a wrong that never should have happened. History is filled with tales of injustice. It is only on rare occasions—with the clarity of hindsight and benefit of careful thought and measured reason—that a society comes together to undo the wrongs of the past.
>
> But make no mistake. It is impossible that with the stroke of a pen, and the granting of a Free Pardon, history is forgotten and the proverbial slate is wiped clean. On the contrary, this very moment in the Viola Desmond story will ensure her legacy lives on in legal journals, in newspapers, in human rights research, in political science debates, and in race relations studies.

This was the first time in Canada's history that the Free Pardon was granted. The Royal Prerogative of Mercy, granting a Free Pardon, can only be executed by the Queen or her representative. And it is only granted to someone who is innocent.

AT THE same ceremony the government issued an apology to Viola's family and to African Nova Scotians. In it, the Premier said, "The arrest, detainment, and conviction of Viola Desmond is an example in our history where the law was used to perpetuate racism and racial segregation. This is contrary to the values of Canadian society" (*Halifax Herald*, April 16, 2010).

What happened to Viola changed her life. I cannot help but think about what could have been. As I said in my speech at the launch of the *Viola Desmond* ferry on June 19, 2016:

> *Unfortunately, we will never know to what heights Viola would have taken her business. Did that cruel act on November 8, 1946, and its aftermath break her spirit and crush her dreams? Viola was attempting to grow her business. Imagine for a moment, the empire she could have built. Imagine how her successful business could have contributed to the economy and cultural fabric of this city, country, and province. Imagine the number of girls, especially Black girls and yes, Black boys, she could have inspired. I know she inspired my dear friend and mentor the late Beverly Mascoll, who began her successful journey into the world of the beauty business. Beverly became a multi-millionaire. Viola was her inspiration.*

Many people have asked if I thought Viola's pardon would have taken place had the government not changed. That question I cannot answer, and I care not to speculate. The NDP government did the right thing by ensuring that justice was served by recognizing

*In April 2010, Lieutenant-Governor Mayann Francis executed the Royal
Prerogative of Mercy to grant posthumously a Free Pardon to Viola Desmond.*
(PROVINCE OF NOVA SCOTIA)

*Mayann Francis signs the Royal Prerogative of Mercy granting a Free Pardon
to Viola Desmond. From left, Desmond's sister, Wanda Robson, looks on,
along with Premier Darrell Dexter, the Honourable Percy Paris, and Attorney
General and Justice Minister Ross Landry.* (PROVINCE OF NOVA SCOTIA)

Viola's innocence. I would like to believe that all governments, regardless of political party, would recognize that the *Canadian Charter of Rights and Freedoms* is entrusted to them. As such they are responsible for ensuring that the rights of all individuals are protected, even if the injustice took place many years ago.

The provincial Progressive Conservative government did table a bill following the Free Pardon, which proposed November 8 as a day to be observed in Viola Desmond's name. The Honourable Percy Paris, who was at the time the NDP's minister of African Nova Scotian Affairs and who had previously raised concerns about racism within the provincial legislature, voiced his objection to their proposal when he stood in the legislature and made these comments, published in the *Halifax Herald* on April 16, 2010:

> *On a day when we all should be proud, trying to rush a bill through the House without consultation from the Black community is not the right thing to do. I think it would be disrespectful, of every member of this House, to rush this bill through without having a vehicle, an opportunity for people from the community to have their say.*

It is my understanding that all three parties would have supported the bill. I believe Mr. Paris's objection was the reason the bill did not become a reality. In 2015 Nova Scotia instituted a new holiday called Nova Scotia Heritage Day, celebrated on the third Monday in February. The idea is that every year the holiday celebrates a different honouree. A list of honourees was created and Viola Desmond was selected as the first.

The connection between Viola and myself cannot be denied. I, a Black woman, freed another Black woman who was falsely accused and convicted for taking a stand against racism and discrimination. The last paragraph of an article published in the *Calgary Herald* on April 20, 2010, titled "Fitting Tribute to Ugly Chapter," says,

The crowning satisfaction and one which shows just how far society has evolved since those long ago days when things were, literally, a matter of black and white is that Lt. Gov. Mayann Francis signed Desmond's pardon. Francis is Black. There's a marvellous sense that the circle is complete.

The Viola Desmond story was not widely known before her Free Pardon in 2010; now it is. Granting Viola her freedom ensured that Viola and the injustice she suffered would never be forgotten. Viola was inducted posthumously into Canada's Walk of Fame on November 15, 2017, and in 2018 she became the first woman and first person of colour to be on the Canadian currency. One of the ferries that runs between Dartmouth and Halifax now bears her name. Ryerson University holds an annual Viola Desmond Award Ceremony; 2018 was the tenth anniversary for this celebration. There are four awards—faculty award, student award, staff award, and high school student award—each named after a "strong Black woman." The 2018 student award was named the Honourable Mayann Francis Ryerson Student Award, which I was honoured to present in person. And in October 2018 I was invited by Dalhousie University to emcee the inaugural Viola Desmond Legacy Lecture at the Belong Forum, which featured American author and professor Angela Davis, who has advocated for social justice since the 1960s. Dal's four-year Viola Desmond Lecture Series celebrates diversity and inclusiveness.

Viola is buried in Camp Hill Cemetery, which is next door to my current residence. I became aware of her final resting place years after I signed the Free Pardon. I approached my City Councillor, Waye Mason, who was unaware that Viola was buried there. Thanks to the assistance of municipal staff, Viola's gravesite is now clearly marked and easy for the public to find.

I hope that future generations will see the granting of the Free Pardon as confirmation of the province's attempt to bring in a new era of inclusiveness in Nova Scotia, by admitting that racism and discrimination did exist and are unfortunately still part of our society today. It is only by acknowledging the past and the injustices of the present that progress will be made when it comes to the full and equal treatment for all citizens.

AS I worked on this memoir, I wondered how I could capture the joy of living in Government House. Living in that beautiful, majestic, historic home made me wish to share it with the public. It was always my wish for Government House to have a warm and welcoming atmosphere for everyone who passed through its doors. In 2010, I initiated a public lecture series. I thought this would be an excellent way for the public to have access to Government House. All lectures were delivered by Nova Scotians and covered a variety of topics. Musical performances also took place, including an opera on November 7, 2010, the first ever to be held in Government House. *Bastien and Bastienne* was produced by Opera Nova Scotia and directed by Dr. Walter Kemp. It was a night to remember.

Another pilot project saw Government House open to the public for guided tours led by provincial government pages from July to August 2011. I cannot help but wonder what additional opportunities I might have created for the public within the walls of the vice-regal residence had I been a resident of Government House for my entire tenure. Government House is still open for public tours, which have been expanded, and monthly public lectures still take place.

One other lasting contribution I made was to change and institutionalize a new emblem for the Office of Lieutenant Governor of Nova Scotia. This emblem brought the office in line with other provincial vice-regal offices. In 2007 the official emblem for the Office was completed and recorded in Ottawa by the Canadian Heraldic Authority. Also during my tenure, in 2011 the cipher worn by aides-de-camp in Nova Scotia was officially recorded by the authority.

By the time my tenure was over, Government House, under the guidance of the private secretary, was operating efficiently. People often asked about the valuable items in Government House. Inventory of the contents in Government House is done by the Transportation & Infrastructure Renewal Inventory Control Group at the start and end of the mandate for each lieutenant-governor. In January 2012, while I was still in office, there was a request made to the private secretary to arrange a time to update the inventory at Government House. When I was made aware that the inventory would include the private quarters, I questioned why. The response to the private secretary was interesting. An email dated January 24, 2012, stated: "The intent was that we would have an inventory of the items prior to Her Honour going and then review it again after she was gone and before a new LG comes in to occupy the building. As a result of issues of items being removed during the exit of an LG, we have [done this] for the last couple of LGs."

As soon as the request came to inventory the private quarters I reached out to a former lieutenant-governor's wife and a former lieutenant-governor, each of whom told me that to their knowledge inventory of the private quarters was not done while they were still in office. One said, "We just packed up and left."

I was uncomfortable with the request because in my view, the inventory should have been done at the start of my mandate in 2006, before they closed the residence, and again prior to my move into the residence on December 11, 2010. My recollection was that before the house closed, an inventory was done. I said I'd like a letter from the deputy minister requesting access to the private quarters. No request came. I did, however, have a meeting with the deputy minister where I expressed my concern. Inventory was not taken of the private quarters while I was still in residence. My mandate ended in April 2012, two months after their original request. I can only assume that an inventory was taken after I departed. (I should note that because 2011 was proclaimed by the United Nations General Assembly as the

International Year for People of African Descent, I asked the Prime Minister to extend my term until 2012. I did not want my tenure to end during that special year. My request was granted.)

For me the issue of the inventory was about trust. I believed those who made the request were questioning my honesty and my integrity. Maybe this was not their intention. I will never know. For me, it was a difficult pill to swallow. Nonetheless, my spirit was not broken because my faith in God gave me the courage to deny their request and ask questions. This allowed me to move forward with my pride and dignity intact.

> For this reason we never become discouraged. Even though our physical being is gradually decaying, yet our spiritual being is renewed day after day. And this small and temporary trouble we suffer will bring us a tremendous and eternal glory, much greater than the trouble. For we fix our attention not on things that are seen but on things that are unseen. What can be seen only lasts for a time, but what cannot be seen lasts forever. (2 Corinthians 4:16–18)

The people of this province were amazing. They gave me the strength and encouragement, especially during the first three years, that helped me to keep moving forward. I enjoyed going into their communities, welcoming them to Government House, visiting their places of worship, spending time with students, supporting our province's arts and culture community, and so many other important and exciting opportunities that always filled me with pride and excitement.

WHEN I became lieutenant-governor, I was acutely aware that the clothing I wore as the Queen's representative would be closely scrutinized. Now, you could argue that my clothes would be closely watched because I am a woman. Yes, that's true. But the curiosity would be heightened because I am a Black woman, full stop. I had to get it right because I was the first. I was determined that I would fulfill the role with dignity and honour. For me this not only meant my actions and behaviour, it also meant how I dressed for the role. For this, I fell back on the teachings of my parents.

They expected their children to not only be educated, but also that we would carry ourselves with confidence and decorum. Our parents wanted us to give respect and demand respect. My mother often said, "You will be educated, but you must also be ladies." For my mother, how we dressed was top of mind. We had clothes to wear for school, clothes to play in, and clothes for Sunday worship. We certainly were not wealthy, but we were always dressed appropriately for various occasions. It helped that my mom made most of our clothes.

My mother's views on how to dress influenced my life. When I went for interviews for positions, I put thought into what I should wear. For every job interview, I wore a suit and a blouse that did not reveal any cleavage, and I made certain that my skirt did not cling to my body. My hemline was always below the knee. I refused to play into any preconceptions the interview panel might have about Black women. On the job I continued the principles I set for myself about my dress.

My designer while in office was Salwa Majaess, who had been highly recommended to me by my friend Daurene Lewis, former mayor of Annapolis Royal and the first Black female mayor in Canada. Daurene had used Salwa on many occasions to make her clothes for special events. Salwa, proprietor of Etalier Salwa, is a Lebanese Canadian who understood why I had to get "the dress" right. From the selection of material, colour, style, hemline, and neckline, we discussed and analyzed the relevance of each item.

After my tenure ended in 2012, I had the idea to share with the public my wardrobe as lieutenant-governor and the story behind each garment, but I wasn't sure how to go about it. An idea came to me after a visit to England in 2014. I discovered there were numerous museums that housed the clothing of historical figures both past and present. It excited me to think about the many stories from Nova Scotia's history that could be told through clothing and textiles, especially because people from different cultures have contributed to our life as a province. Clothing is a different lens through which we can learn about our collective history. Can you imagine a museum in Nova Scotia that housed garments and textiles of historical figures past and present and the stories behind these items? Think what we could learn about the individuals and our society. I hoped that if I had an exhibition about my clothing, a conversation could begin about the viability of having such a museum in Nova Scotia.

Peter Dykhuis, director/curator of Dalhousie Art Gallery, was interested in my idea. My dream became a reality in 2016, a few years after our initial conversation. Not only would I be sharing with the public the garments I wore as lieutenant-governor and the story behind each outfit, but the gallery space/exhibition would be shared with Shauntay Grant, lecturer in Dalhousie's Department of English, spoken word artist, author, and former Halifax poet laureate. Her exhibition, *Stitched Stories*, which she curated herself, displayed quilts made by her grandmother. Every quilt has a unique history and story. Shauntay is a descendant of Black Loyalists, Black refugees, and Jamaican Maroons who arrived in Canada during the eighteenth and nineteenth centuries. The two exhibitions opened in September 2016.

Along with Paige Connell and Angela A. Glanzmann, employees of Dalhousie Art Gallery, and Gary Markle, fashion instructor at the Nova Scotia College of Art and Design, I curated my exhibition, *The Dress: Mayann Francis, The Call to Serve.* We displayed the formal Civil Uniform worn during the Speech from the Throne, gowns, suits, shoes, dresses, jewellery, purses, hats, and hairstyles.

This, in part, is how the exhibition was advertised:

Reflecting back on her years of service as the Queen's represen-
tative to the province, Francis underscores how the garments
that she wore communicated the presence and the dignity of her
office. To this end, rather than purchase off-the-rack garments,
Francis often actively worked with Halifax-based designer
Etalier Salwa to author the appropriate silhouette, fabric choices,
hats, jewellery, and accessories, to set a stylish but respectful
tone for the many formal events that she was scheduled to attend
in her vice-regal capacity.

[...]

Francis's personal stories interweave throughout the exhi-
bition to highlight how the politics of fabrics and garments can
also respectively play with the politics of public events, regal
positions, and pomp and circumstance.

I was excited by the interest demonstrated by the public, media, and art students in *The Dress*. On November 15, Gary Markle and I recorded an interview that was aired on *q*, CBC Radio's popular arts and entertainment show. We were thrilled. They wanted to highlight particular outfits, like what I wore when I signed the Royal Prerogative of Mercy Free Pardon for Viola Desmond, my installation outfit, and the outfit I wore to greet Her Majesty when she arrived at Government House in June 2010. They were also very interested in hearing from Gary about the significance of garments/ textiles to history, and the psychological and philosophical reasons behind people's fashion choices.

I delivered a public lecture on the issues that influenced my choice of clothing, and Gary and I also spoke to the *Coast*, Halifax's free alternative weekly newspaper, about the exhibition. In the September 29, 2016, edition Morgan Mullin writes, "As both Francis and Markle explain, typically textile archives act as a way to permeate into the quotidian of the past." The article continues,

A lack of a textile archive in Nova Scotia means a lack of touch-able history. The Dress *is a way to address that void, while also broaching some of the topics on Francis's mind around her position and wardrobe.*" She then quotes me saying, "I had to get it right, that's all there was to it.... It was also about the politics behind the selection of the type of dress you'd wear. I'm bringing the whole issue of gender, class, and race and how that affects the whole thought process about the garment.

Home is where the heart is. When I go down memory lane my heart is often in Whitney Pier, depending upon the factors that trigger my thoughts of home. Some of my garments did that, especially the hats, gloves, and purses, because this is how our family dressed when we attended church. When I wore those garments, I felt a strengthening of my spirituality; the church and my belief in God were the foundation of my journey in public life.

The Dress: Mayann Francis and the Call to Serve closed in November 2016. I was honoured to have had the opportunity to display the garments and to tell the stories behind them. I was called to serve. As the first Black person to be called to this high office in Nova Scotia, I wanted to leave behind a legacy of honour, goodness, peace, and hope. My "dress" and the story behind it played a major part in my journey as the Queen's representative. A member of the public phoned to say that the exhibition gave her hope.

As the article in the *Coast* concluded,

To see the cloth collaborations of a Lebanese-Canadian designer and an African Nova Scotian lieutenant-governor is to see something bigger than a study in classical tailoring. It's an archive of textiles, yes, and also an archive of surpassing the expectations of stereotypes, one three-buttoned jacket at a time.

When my tenure as lieutenant-governor ended on April 12, 2012, with the swearing-in of Brigadier-General John James Grant, CMM, CD (retired), I presented the Royal Key to His Honour. After that symbolic gesture, a feeling of peace and contentment consumed me. I was proud of what I had accomplished. As many people have said, I came to the office with a unique and wide perspective because of my background in human rights, human resources, religious studies, public administration, health, and law. Collectively my background gave me the ability to feel comfortable with a wide range of people and enjoy their company. My hope is that my actions as lieutenant-governor demonstrated my deep respect for my province and its citizens.

Chapter II

REFLECTIONS ON RACE AND RACISM, THE JOURNEY, AND LESSONS LEARNED

No dear brothers and sisters, I have not achieved it, but I focus on this one thing: forgetting the past and looking forward to what lies ahead, I press on to reach the end of the race and receive the heavenly prize for which God, through Christ Jesus, is calling us.

PHILIPPIANS 3:13–14

It has been over a decade since I took the Oath of Office. Sometimes it seems like yesterday. During my first year out of office, I often took time to reflect on the role I played. Even though my first three years were difficult and painful, I treasure the collective memories of my time as lieutenant-governor.

Once when I was giving a private tour to a military officer and his family, I was surprised when he commented on the lack of diversity on the walls. He said, "Everyone is white." (By the way, he was white.) I was happy he noticed and that he was sensitive to the fact that history is not complete when part of the story remains untold. African Nova Scotian history and Mi'kmaw history have been excluded or inaccurately portrayed. One of my goals before I concluded my time as lieutenant-governor was to change the walls of Government House by breaking the colour barrier.

A portrait of Chief Membertou by Alan Syliboy, a highly respected and well-known Mi'kmaw artist, was presented to Her Majesty during her 2010 visit. The painting was gifted back to the Mi'kmaw people, then was subsequently gifted to Government House where it is now prominently displayed.

A painting of William Hall, the first Black Nova Scotian and first Black Canadian to receive the Victoria Cross, and portraits of Viola Desmond and myself, now grace the walls of Government House. With the exception of Queen Charlotte's, our portraits were the first in recent history to add colour to the walls of Government House.

Portia White, a world-renowned African Nova Scotian contralto born in Halifax, broke the colour barrier in the Canadian classical music industry. She performed for Her Majesty in Prince Edward Island in 1964. Portia White's portrait was donated to Government House after my tenure concluded.

I should also mention that at the time my portrait was being painted and sponsored through the generous donation and kindness of Larry Gibson, a successful Black Halifax businessman, I asked him if he would also financially support a portrait to be painted of my predecessor, the Honourable Myra Freeman, the first female lieutenant-governor and first Jewish person to be appointed vice-regal representative. Her portrait is also now displayed in Government House.

Being the Queen's representative allowed me to experience what it was like to go into a store and not be followed or ignored. It was such a feeling of freedom. If I went into a store while in office, the driver was never far away from me. People connected the dots and realized who I was. So they did not ignore me and neither did they follow me. Prior to my appointment to this high office, I put much thought into entering certain stores. I know it sounds crazy, but I did my best to minimize the possibility of being accused of stealing. If I was carrying a knapsack, I made certain all zippers were closed. If I was carrying a bag, I usually put it in my knapsack. I never opened my knapsack until I reached the checkout. If my cellphone rang, rest assured I would not answer it, because it meant going into my knapsack or my pocket.

In April 2015 I took a public stand against racial profiling of people who were shopping. I felt it was important that I stand with the Black community to protest the injustice of racial profiling. I have been a victim of "shopping while Black" racial profiling both before and after I left the office of lieutenant-governor. People expressed shock and disbelief that such racist behaviour could happen to me. As long as my skin is black, it does not matter what heights I achieve; somewhere along the journey the ugly head of racism and discrimination will surface. It manifests itself in different ways.

When I went public about my experiences, some people behaved just as I expected they would. I received calls from people who said they were discriminated against because their hair is now grey. They found they were ignored when they went into a store. I do not doubt their story. Nonetheless, they were unknowingly minimizing the validity of my experience. In my opinion, they were in denial that racism is alive and well. When they were revealing their experience, I kept thinking, "You could just dye your hair or put on a wig. I can dye my hair, put on a wig, but guess what? I cannot dye my face." And if this is their only experience of being ignored, because their hair is grey, I wonder how or if they would have survived had they lived their life as a Black person.

Of course, racial profiling is not confined to shopping, it also happens while driving. Many Black people, especially Black men, can recount stories about being pulled over by the police for unexplained reasons. A Black friend of mine, who drives a rather nice vehicle, shared his experience about being stopped. He slowed down to pass by an accident, then picked up his speed again. Next thing he knew he was pulled over for driving erratically! And of course, there's the Kirk Johnson case. As I mentioned when recounting my time as head of the Nova Scotia Human Rights Commission, in December 2003, the commission's Board of Inquiry ruled that race was indeed a factor when police stopped Mr. Johnson and impounded his vehicle. The ruling raised the profile of racial profiling in Nova Scotia and beyond.

Racial profiling can occur anywhere. I know this from personal experience. On August 23, 2016, I was travelling with a tour group on a day excursion on board the Bernina Express train in Europe. We boarded in Tiefencastel, Switzerland, heading to Tirano, Italy. We had a car reserved for our group. The tour manager reminded us to travel with our passports. She added that in her experience, it was highly unlikely we would be asked to produce our passport at the border. When we reached Italy, no one was asked to produce their passport. There were about forty of us in the group. I was the only Black person.

Shortly after we boarded the train in Tirano for the return trip to Switzerland, the conductor stamped our special Swiss Transfer Travel Ticket. I was sitting alone near the door across from two friends at the back of the reserved car. Looking out the window at the Alps, I was lost in the beauty and the splendour of what I was seeing. I was in awe.

Suddenly a man in uniform was standing over me. He was not speaking English, but I knew he wanted to see my passport. I handed him my Canadian passport, but he kept asking me questions. Because I did not know what he was asking, I kept repeating my name, where I was from, and that I was a tourist. My friends had their passports in hand, ready for examination. Even though I did not fully understand what he was asking me, I knew I had to stay calm and cooperate. I remember looking at his eyes. Even though he was courteous, his eyes were empty. I did my best not to show nervousness, disrespect, or anger. After all, he had the power to remove me from the train and detain me; this was my fear. Finally, after what seemed like an eternity, he handed me my passport and left.

My friends sat there with their mouths open. "He went to you because of your colour!" They were in disbelief. I said, "Welcome to my world." You see, my friends had heard about discrimination and racism or read about it, but I do not believe they had ever witnessed it first-hand.

Within minutes of this episode, the train stopped at the next station, where the border guard left the train and got into a waiting vehicle. My friend's husband took a photo of him getting into the car. Meanwhile my friend called the tour manager and related the story. The manager said she saw him come into the car, but she thought he was just walking through. I said, "Yes, he was. He was walking straight through to me." She immediately went to the conductor and told him what happened. Reportedly, he said, "That's the way things are in Europe now." She demanded he apologize to me. As he was walking past my seat, I stopped him and asked why I was the only person in this special car to be singled out. He confirmed what he had told the tour manager. I asked if he meant I was targeted because of my skin colour. He said yes, apologized, and quickly walked away.

Needless to say, I was sad and angry for the balance of the trip. My peace was gone. And my friends were having a difficult time with what they had witnessed. I wondered how the border security knew I was on the train. Did they follow me onto the train in Italy, or were they alerted by the conductor and boarded the train shortly after we left Italy? Or were they already on the train and told by the conductor which car I was on? I will never know. What I can say for certain is that I was racially profiled. Little did I know when the Ambassador of Switzerland paid a courtesy call to me in 2007 when I was lieutenant-governor that I would experience racial profiling in his country in 2016. I am glad I did not have a crystal ball.

When I related the story to my aerobics group in Halifax upon my return, one of them, a white woman, looked at me and quietly said, "You must get tired?" I replied, "Yes, I do." Even on vacation, my peace was taken away from me.

When I returned to Canada, I filed a complaint with the Swiss Embassy in Ottawa. My letter was forwarded to the Swiss Border Guards in Switzerland. The response to my letter from the commander of the border guard region was disturbing. In part the letter dated October 28, 2016, stated,

> *The allegations you made against our employees have thus been examined carefully and extensively. The current refugee situation on the African continent and the migratory pressure on Switzerland's southern border resulting from this has forced us to carry out targeted people checks in spite of limited resources. Our employees carry out checks based on situation and risk analyses.*

It further stated,

> *In this case the inspecting border officer was unaware before the check was carried out that this was a special travel group. Unfortunately, it has increasingly happened in recent weeks that refugees mingled with tourists. This trend continued over the past few days as we were examining your allegations. It*

*is for this reason that you were subjected to a brief but cour-
teous check. The border police officer terminated the check
immediately when your nationality became apparent. We
categorically reject the allegation of racial profiling against
our employee.*

In my opinion, their letter confirmed my allegations of racial
profiling. Because I am Black, they assumed I was an African
migrant. I was prompted to hire the services of one of the best law
firms in Halifax, known internationally and renowned for securing
letters of apology for discriminatory behaviour such as I had experienced in Switzerland. They drafted a letter in response to the one
I had received from the border guard, saying,

*While you state that it is ethically unacceptable to check travel-
lers based on their skin colour and reject any allegation of racial
profiling, your subsequent assumption that Her Honour could be
a danger or a refugee 'mingled with tourists' was only based on
her skin colour and the possibility that she was from the African
continent. There were no other circumstances that created any
element of risk that justified her being singled out in the fashion
she was.*

The law firm's letter went on to provide the Merriam-Webster
dictionary definition of profiling as "the act of suspecting or target-
ing a person on the basis of observed characteristics or behaviour."
Further, "racial profiling would therefore be the suspecting or tar-
geting of a person on the basis of their race or skin colour," something their letter admitted to.

I received my letter of apology. Some people felt I should have
asked for monetary compensation. I was not interested in their
money. For me it was about my dignity and my satisfaction that
my complaint was heard and validated.

My experience reminded me of the time in 2013 when a clerk in a Swiss shop refused to show Oprah a purse valued at $38,000. When Oprah discussed what happened to her on television, the explanations and apologies came quickly. They realized they had racially profiled one of the richest persons in the world. As in many cases of racism and discrimination, the perpetrator will try to justify their behaviour with excuses. In Oprah's case, the boutique owner referred to the incident as a "misunderstanding." In my case it was the excuse of an African migrant problem. Even though I was sitting in a private car with other tourists, I couldn't possibly be a tourist because my skin was black; hence, I was suspect.

I cannot overstate that no matter how successful or prominent or wealthy a Black person becomes, at some point along their journey the pain and humiliation of racism and discrimination will rear its ugly face. What's important is how the assault on one's dignity is handled. You must decide whether to fight or absorb the pain. To my Black brothers and sisters, speaking from decades of experience, I say never allow these actions to break your spirit. Climb over the barrier, be strong, be steadfast, move on, and learn from the experience. The lessons learned will prepare you for when racism rears its ugly head again. Unfortunately, it will.

When my tenure as lieutenant-governor ended, I did not have fear or concern about letting go or what to do with my life. I left the club to which only a few people can say they belonged. For me it was about giving thanks, resting my soul and my spirit, because I was entering another phase of my journey. I knew God had a plan for what I call my final leg of the journey of life. All I needed to do was still my mind, give thanks, and listen for His call. As is written in the book of Joshua 1:9, "Have I commanded you? Be strong and of good courage: do not be afraid, nor be dismayed, for the Lord your God is with you wherever you go."

There is an old adage that says when one door closes another one opens. Sometimes we do not recognize or do not want to recognize when opportunity knocks. One of the biggest challenges to taking on new opportunities can be fear. We must have the courage to walk through the door when it opens. Before walking through the open door, we should objectively evaluate whether or not this is the door for us. Maybe there is an inner door inside the open door waiting for us. If we decide not to walk through the open door, we must understand the reason behind our decision.

One afternoon, while in office and still living in my condo, I was walking with author and singer Clary Croft and his wife, Sharon. As we neared the railway station, I told them about our family train trips when I was a child, from Cape Breton to New York. Clary commented that my story would make a nice children's book. A few years later, he introduced me to his publisher. I subsequently reached out to Susan Tooke, well-known children's illustrator, for advice, which proved to be very helpful. Even though the door had opened for me to write a children's book, my first response was no way! After all, what do I know about writing for children? I had written many articles and speeches but never a story for children. What if I was rejected? I soon realized I was afraid. I have always been someone who advocated conquering fear. Now it was time for me to practise what I preach. Fortunately, there were friends, acquaintances, and writers who encouraged me to take the leap. I took a deep breath and jumped head-first into the world of writing. I am so glad I did. *Mayann's Train Ride*, illustrated by Tamara Thiebaux Heikalo and published by Nimbus in 2015, is the result of walking through the open door of opportunity and possibilities. It wasn't easy, but I did it. In 2018 it was translated into French, *Mayann prend le train*.

I want to share with you another story about conquering fear. When my role as lieutenant-governor ended in April 2012, I decided to take time to reflect on the experience. This did not mean that I would sit with my feet up every day. No, I was interested in staying active through exercise. I joined a walking group, and it is a privilege to be one of their members. We meet every Saturday morning and walk with our Nordic poles. If we do not walk (due to snow and ice) we meet anyway for coffee and conversation. I also joined an aerobics group called Forever Fit. Joining both groups has giving me the pleasure of meeting wonderful and interesting women. (There are a few men in the aerobics group who are also very nice.) In both groups, most if not all of us are retired but still active either serving on boards, travelling around the world, hiking, doing volunteer work...I could go on and on.

One day at our Forever Fit class, a few members who were on the board of Live Art Dance approached me. They asked me if I would take part in their fundraiser, which included the "Dancing with the Halifamous" competition, where famous people were partnered with choreographers or professional dancers to compete with one another. First I thought they were joking. Me, on stage, dancing in front of an audience? I don't think so. Yes, I can speak in front of large crowds, but to actually dance onstage? No way!

I was asked to think about it because it was for a good cause. They approached me a couple of times. I finally gave in, telling myself to conqueror my fear. Be brave, Mayann. Just do it.

I was partnered with musical theatre artist Kristen Howell. A song from the musical *Chicago* was choreographed for the two of us by Alexis Milligan. I was a nervous wreck. How could I completely transform myself and dance? I went to all the rehearsals and yes, I practiced at home every day. My precious cat, Angel, watched me very closely. If only I could have read her mind.

When the night came for us to perform, March 9, 2013, I convinced myself to get out there, relax, and remember to play the role of a skilled dancer and actor. In other words, I was not Mayann Francis. I gave it my all, doing moves that even surprised me. Oh well, I was someone else.

Guess what? We won! We were named the 2013 Halifamous Dance Champions. I have to say, it was fun and I am glad I took the leap. I conquered my fear and doubt.

Much of my life has been about coming full circle. I worked as a human rights officer in the early 1970s, then two decades later became the CEO and executive director of the Nova Scotia Human Rights Commission. A circle I did not expect to complete was the appointment by Dalhousie University to the Faculty of Management, School of Public Administration as their first distinguished public service fellow in the fall of 2015. I was Dalhousie's first employment equity officer in the early 1990s. Another circle closed.

My appointment was both exciting and terrifying. I have a tremendous respect for academics. They spent a great deal of their life studying, conducting research, and becoming experts in their field of study. They are valuable contributors to our communities, locally, nationally, and internationally. I guess I wondered if I would fit in. The door was wide open, so I decided to enter the open door and I am happy I did.

In the first public lecture I delivered as part of my duties as distinguished fellow, I told the story of my journey to Government House. I wanted my appointment to Dalhousie to be seen as a sign of hope for anyone who has faced countless barriers in their life. I was a long way from my humble beginnings in Whitney Pier, Cape Breton. I owed the march forward not only to myself but also to my ancestors who struggled to survive the brutal legacy of slavery. The oppressor succeeded in convincing the world that we were inferior, we were animals, and stereotypes about Black people perpetuate these myths. Even though strides have been made, African Canadians are still under-represented in many aspects of our society, like membership on corporate boards, the upper ranks of the federal, provincial, and municipal public service, political office, senior levels in universities, the health sector, the media, the justice system...I could go on.

Tony Ince, an African Nova Scotian, was elected to the Nova Scotia Legislature in 2013 and served as minister of Communities, Culture, and Heritage. In 2017 he was appointed minister of the

Public Service Commission, and he is also minister of African Nova Scotian Affairs. Will he be able to change the face of the senior levels of the provincial public service? He may have the will and desire to bring about change, but he will also need the strong support of bureaucrats and politicians.

Pointing to the fact that 2015 to 2024 has been proclaimed by the United Nations as the International Decade for People of African Descent, in 2018 Nova Scotia's premier, Stephen McNeil, reaffirmed his government's commitment to address systemic racism and discrimination to ensure that no citizen is judged or held back because of who they are. Currently, I am not aware of any African Canadians or other visible minorities at the deputy or assistant deputy minister level in Nova Scotia. I believe the last African Canadian senior level official to serve as deputy minister was Gordon Earle, who was DM of the Department of Housing and Consumer Affairs well over a decade ago, the first African Nova Scotian to serve in this capacity; and of course, I had deputy head status as CEO and executive director of the Nova Scotia Human Rights Commission, but I left over twelve years ago, in 2006.

Will civil servants accept, respect, cooperate with, and support an African Nova Scotian or racial minority as deputy or assistant deputy minister? Will they trust and accept advice from a non-white deputy minister? Lack of acceptance based on race is in my view one of the barriers we face as a Black race, even in organizations that appear to be welcoming. Bringing about change at the senior ranks and throughout the public service will not be easy. Nonetheless, I believe that with honesty, dedication, commitment, and determination, change is possible.

Governments should be working with universities that offer programs in public administration to develop short- and long-term strategies to achieve a diverse workforce. Universities and governments should increase their outreach to communities, especially African Nova Scotian communities, to promote career opportunities in government and how a university education in public administration could help. The corporate community could do similar outreach for their own businesses and organizations.

The immigrant population in the Maritimes and Canada is rapidly growing, and the Aboriginal population is the fastest growing in Canada. In 2015 Statistics Canada projected that by 2017, the Aboriginal population would increase to approximately 1.4 million. The time to strategize about change and inclusion is now, not tomorrow.

Progress will truly be demonstrated when a Black Nova Scotian, racial minority, or First Nations individual is appointed as deputy minister or assistant deputy minister of a line department and not DM or ADM responsible for diversity and inclusion. Not that there is anything wrong with such an appointment. It is, however, too easy for businesses and governments to bolster their minority employment equity statistics at senior levels when racial minorities occupy these roles with very little or no opportunity to move into wider policy roles or other areas that would help them move into positions that could give them the experience needed to climb the corporate and/or government ladder. Governments or corporations could use these appointments as an opportunity to prepare individuals with the potential to grow and take on other management roles that would set them on a path of upward mobility.

Of course, it does not do anyone any good to appoint someone without the necessary qualifications, regardless of level or position. "Window dressing" harms not only the individual but the organization as well. It can lead to the belief that organizations that strive for inclusion have lowered their standards. This is a myth that must be debunked. Individuals, regardless of who they are, must be hired or promoted because they are qualified for the job.

If their goal is to have a workforce that is inclusive, not exclusive, organizations, whether government, not-for profit, private industry, or universities, must continuously review their human resources and employment equity policies. To be effective, policy development and delivery of services must include a diverse team of people not only at senior levels but also throughout the bureaucracy. How effective are the policies and strategies to bring about lasting change? How will these strategies be evaluated? How will the outcomes be measured? These policies must not be reviewed independent of one another—they are inextricably linked. Recruitment initiatives should include outreach to targeted communities. Did the outreach yield positive results? Is retention a problem? If so, why? Are there "glass ceilings" or other barriers that prevent upward mobility or access? Is the environment a welcoming one? What is the union's position when it comes to equity, upward mobility, and protection of seniority? How many complaints were related to human rights? Do training agendas include educational programs on diversity and inclusivity? What does accountability look like? How often are programs assessed for their effectiveness? Organizations seeking to diversify must prepare the environment for the acceptance of change as it relates to equity groups.

As someone who has worked in private industry and at senior levels of government, I can testify that the challenge is real. As a Black person, I had to work harder than anyone else. It may not be fair, but until our society becomes fully inclusive, that's the way it is. I had to develop strategies and a thick skin just for survival in some instances. The first strategy is know your job and much more. Never stop learning. Read everything you need to know about your role, and if you report to someone, learn his or her job. Understand as much as you can about leadership.

Be aware of your surroundings. Know the difference between your true allies and those who pretend to be your ally. Have your trusted advisors, both internally and externally, with whom you can bounce ideas and vent when you have to. Make sure your advisors are a diverse group, not only in colour and orientation but also people who have something positive to offer you.

My advisors were a mixture of business and government leaders, grassroots people, financially successful people, and people from various professional backgrounds, different colours, different religions, and different ages. Each person contributed to my growth and understanding of people, what leadership means in a working environment. They taught me the value of discernment and how important it is to be an active listener. These lessons, along with my education and my own common sense, helped me chart a course of success.

Communicating with a variety of people and keeping the lines of communications open to new learning is always important, regardless of where you might be employed or what level you are at in the organization. CEOs have to be great communicators as well.

Never comprise your integrity or dignity. Make transparency and accountability your best friends. Stay humble.

Know when to absorb the pain of some negative situations. There will always be comments made that are insensitive or an attempt to make you react in such a way that could cost you your job or your reputation. These remarks can be deliberate or due to ignorance. Remember, as a Black person one mistake could wipe out your years of hard work. You will be remembered for how you responded.

Here is an example of being tested on this last point. A politician asked me a foolish question after I had signed the Free Pardon for Viola Desmond. I am not certain if they realized the magnitude of their question. First the person applauded that I had pardoned Viola. Then, out of nowhere, they asked if Viola was related to me. In my view the question was out of line. First of all, if I were related to Ms. Desmond, it certainly would not be anything that I would want to hide. I would have expressed my delight publicly about freeing my relative. And the media would have picked up on this as well. Maybe the individual did not agree with the pardon and wondered if I had pardoned Ms. Desmond because we were related?

If the person had nothing else to say after they expressed their support for Viola's freedom, wouldn't it have been best if they had simply ended the conversation and not tried to make insensitive and foolish small talk? There is a long held misconception that all Blacks look alike, that we know all other Black people, and we are all related. Gee, I wish the latter were true, because then I could claim the Obamas as my family.

I took a deep breath and told the person that we were not related. I bit my tongue and controlled what I really wanted to say. I was not prepared to lose my dignity because of someone else's ignorance.

There will always be foolish comments when people do not know what to say. Take for example the political staffer in Ontario who was so uncomfortable when they first met me that out of nowhere, without any context, they said how much they liked Aretha Franklin. I counted to ten then looked them straight in the eye. "Really?" I said. "I prefer to listen to country and western music." There was an eerie silence. The person did not respond. I wonder why? (By the way, I am a fan of Aretha Franklin.)

Sometimes these foolish comments arise because the individual has never had a conversation with someone who is from a different cultural or racial background. I certainly have had experience talking with people who have never talked to a person from another cultural group. I hear the common story, the remarks about suntans that many Black people prepare themselves for. You know, the constant comparing of their tanned white skin to yours. "Gee, I am almost as dark as you. Do you burn or tan?" Well, as a Black person you can either suck it up or ask them if they have read *Black Like Me*, first published in 1961, by white journalist John Howard Griffin. Mr. Griffin wanted to experience what it was like to live as a Black man in the southern United States. He darkened his skin to pass for black. It is safe to say that his very negative experiences surprised him.

Throughout her life, Mayann Francis has changed her hairstyle to suit her mood and the occasion. At one point, she sported a striking short blonde hairdo.
(COURTESY OF AUTHOR)

And I cannot forget what I call one of a Black woman's most important accessories—her hair. Throughout my life I have changed my hairstyle, not only to suit my mood, but also for the occasion and for what I was wearing. I have gone from short black afro to blonde afro; straight hair to curly; braids to dreadlocks; and from short hair to shoulder-length hair in twenty-four hours. Throughout my journey with the changing hair accessory, my one rule is, do not touch my hair. That's a no, no. Most Black women, if not all, do not want you to touch their hair, unless of course you are their stylist. You can admire or not admire. Just don't touch without permission. Chris Rock's 2009 documentary *Good Hair* shines a light on the sensitivity of Black women's hair.

As someone who has a record of being the first, I was well aware that I was a proxy for all Black people. If I messed up it might be years, or maybe never, before another Black person would be hired again. When I was leaving one position, a senior person who was distraught that I was leaving expressed their desire to fill the spot with another Black person exactly like me, and could I recommend someone. I am not an identical twin, so I could not help them.

I do not think the majority of people who make these remarks mean any harm. I also believe that many people do not understand when a Black person might take offense to something that was said. I don't believe they understand that these actions for many Black people are annoying, insensitive, and not funny. Most of the times, though, I have experienced open, honest, and pleasant conversations with people who were comfortable with themselves and with talking to someone who did not look like them. They clearly wanted to understand why I may have found their behaviour hurtful and insensitive. I liked these conversations because they were always about learning and self-examination.

All human beings have been socialized in many different ways, none of us is perfect. The real test for each of us is knowing when to take a step back and ask ourselves difficult questions that we might prefer not to deal with. It is about being open, honest, and sensitive to other people who come from cultural backgrounds that are different than our own.

Chapter 12

ANCHORS

Fear not, for I am with you. Be not dismayed, for I am your God. I will strengthen you. Yes, I will help you, I will uphold you with My righteous right Hand.

ISAIAH 41:10

In June of 2017, I had the honour of hearing Valerie Jarrett, former chief of staff to President Barack Obama, speak at the Black Business Initiative Summit in Halifax. She demonstrated her intelligence and wisdom by offering sound advice and strategies for moving forward. As I was writing my story, I thought about something she said. To paraphrase, she talked about how there comes a time in our professional life that we "absorb the pain." I realized that I had "absorbed the pain" of some of the negative behaviour I experienced throughout my professional and personal journey. I have not revealed how I truly felt until now. As someone once said, one has to know when to stand up and when to sit down. For me, this memoir is about standing up and sharing. It is about lessons to be learned and encouragement to keep moving forward, because we all have a purpose on this earth.

A rare shot of Mayann Francis's family together. Back row, left to right: brother, George Francis; sister Eloise Yvonne Edwards; sister Lady Isabel Waterman; Mayann Francis. Front row, left to right: foster sister Deborah Lynn Marshall; foster brother, Karl Francis Williams; foster sister Donna Lee Marshall. (COURTESY OF AUTHOR)

While my journey through life has been an exciting and successful one, it was and still is about climbing over barriers and having faith in myself that I can succeed. I often talk to people about valley days. These are the days when you feel like you cannot go forward because it seems as though there is nowhere to turn. For me there was always someplace to turn. I turned to prayer. God was my strength and my armour during those dark days and nights. There was always the dawn of a new day because friends, family, and supporters carried me through.

And I cannot forget Angel, my Ragdoll cat, who brought me joy and comfort for the fourteen years we were together. Her death on June 13, 2015, was unexpected. The impact of her transition opened old wounds. She died on the same day as my dad, who died in 1982.

For thirty-four years, I feared June 13, until 2016 when I received an honorary diploma from the Nova Scotia Community College on that date. It was such a happy and special occasion that it made me realize that I had allowed fear to take hold and keep me captive, closing my mind to the possibility that good things can happen on a date that in the past had caused me pain. I am glad that cycle of thinking was finally broken.

Nonetheless, there were many times I wanted to give up. My journey was not without its ups and downs. I had many valley days. Sometimes those feelings of hopelessness and loss were related to work. The feeling of sadness consumed me when I felt personal loss in love or death. I credit my faith for getting me through those difficult times. I have vivid memories of praying endlessly when I was in high school and first year of college. Morning and night I would recite: "Hail Mary full of grace, the Lord is with thee, blessed art thou among women. Blessed is the fruit of thy womb, Jesus. Holy Mary mother of God, pray for us sinners, now and at the hour of our death." I would say this prayer ten times, then I would have a conversation with the Blessed Virgin asking her to intercede for me. I never worried about my grades when I completed my prayers. I knew I would pass, and I did.

As I grew older and faced many challenges, I relied on my faith in God to keep me strong. My belief in God can be traced back to childhood and my African heritage. People like Fredrick Douglass, Nat Turner, Sojourner Truth, and Harriet Tubman risked their lives to free Black people from the bonds of slavery. Throughout their long struggle, Black people relied on their faith in God. They never gave up hope that one day they would reach the Promised Land.

In the research for their 2010 book, *Race and Well-Being: The Lives, Hopes, and Activism of African Canadians*, the six African Canadian authors found, among other things, that faith and spirituality, especially the church, played a major role in helping African Canadians cope with the pain of discrimination. "Some," they said, "submerge themselves in a culture-based spirituality from a positive sense of racial identity."

I have never hidden the fact that I have a strong belief in God. Many people believe that public figures should keep their religious beliefs private. I certainly understand why people would feel this way. There is the fear that a public person might mix church and state. I have always tried not to impose my religious beliefs on anyone or to allow my beliefs to influence public policy. In November 2016, I delivered a public lecture at Dalhousie University titled "Faith and My Very Public Journey" in order to share who and what were the influences early in my life. I hope the following excerpt from that lecture will shed light on my faith journey and my views on spiritual leadership in the public and private sector.

> *My religious upbringing and my faith have helped me manoeuvre the complexities of life. A life that I knew would often be a challenge because of the colour of my skin and the racist behaviour I have faced.*
>
> *Like my ancestors, my spiritual foundation was the rock on which I stood to help chart the course for survival and success. Because of my faith in Christ's teachings and my belief that God loves me, I have the courage, strength, and hope to keep going, practise forgiveness and forge a path for those who will follow me. Prayer is a constant in my life.*
>
> *St. Augustine teaches that the necessity of prayer for perseverance has always been the faith of the church. Just as Jesus went away to lonely places to pray, I find peace, rejuvenation, and strength in my private time with God. Others may describe this quiet time as "being in the moment" and not attach a name to the silence. This is fine, for I am in no way trying to convert anyone to my beliefs or position. For me, nonetheless, that quiet time is with God. This is my strength, this is my armour. "Wherefore take unto you the whole armour of God that ye*

may be able to withstand in the evil day and having done all, to stand" (Ephesians 6:13). This is the armour I need to help me stand tall and take on the responsibilities of leadership whether on a grand or small scale.

As a graduate of the Atlantic School of Theology (I completed a Certificate in Theological Studies in 2003), I learned a valuable lesson about service and leadership. For me, spiritual leadership combined with responsible leadership can be a dynamic duality. As a student, I penned a paper on spiritual leadership in which I remarked how, in the weeks following the tragedy of 9/11, the call for peace, love, healing, and prayer became the public rallying cry. Political leaders of the world called upon religious leaders to pray and to guide the world through this dark period.

I often reflect about the issues that confront us today and the kind of leaders we need to confront climate change, mental health issues, poverty, gender inequality, sexism, racism, sexual harassment, sexual assault, homophobia, discrimination, human rights violations, national security issues, food security, the impacts of new technology, and an aging population, just to name a few.

In the face of all of this, I think we need people who are of ethical and strong moral character. I also want them to be intelligent and strategic thinkers with a vision. But what about spiritual leadership? When I think about spiritual leadership, I often reflect about the people who were strong in their faith, lived a very public life, and left a lasting positive legacy.

People like the Reverend Dr. Martin Luther King Jr., a man whose name is known throughout the world. He was a man who had the courage and conviction to stand and fight for justice and liberty because of his strong faith and vision. Decades after his death his influence is still felt. Excerpts from his "I Have a Dream" speech often form the foundation for discussions about

ways to heal the racial divide. "Faith," he said, "can give us cour-
age to meet the uncertainties of the future. The people are look-
ing for leadership, and if I stand before them without strength
and courage, they too will falter."

In addition to the experiences that have marked the path of my spiritual journey, there are also world figures who inspire me because of their spirituality. These men and women demonstrate strong leadership on the world stage and have had an amazing impact.

Barack Obama is one of the people I look up to and respect. His strength, honesty, courage, respect, love, and commitment to social justice and fairness have demonstrated, in my opinion, a leadership that is based in spirituality. In his speech to the National Prayer Breakfast in Washington, DC, he indicated that he was inspired by faith leaders of the civil rights movement and his mother. He discussed how his mother was a very spiritual person, even though she did not regularly attend church. He said she was guided by the Golden Rule and she impressed upon him values like honesty, hard work, kindness, and fair play. Because of her teachings and the inspiration from faith leaders, he chose a life of service.

Malala Yousafzai, another person I admire, is a fighter who champions the rights of girls and women. She is young woman with faith and courage. Because she is Muslim and believes that girls should have an education, the Taliban in her native Pakistan attempted to kill her in 2012. She survived the attack and continues to speak out and fight for the rights of girls to have an education. The attempt on her life did not stop or discourage her from speaking out for justice. Malala could have hate in her heart; instead she has forgiven the man who tried to end her life.

Queen Elizabeth II is another individual I admire and respect, and I was deeply honoured to be awarded the Queen's Golden Jubilee Medal in 2002 and the Diamond Jubilee Medal in 2012.

In *The Servant Queen and the King She Serves*, authors Catherine Butcher and Mark Greene say this about Her Majesty: "As a woman of faith she attends church weekly, even on holidays, and prays daily but never tells anyone to go to church. She has no power to make political decisions, but her personal authority has brought nations together." In her 2002 Christmas message, the Queen provided an answer for those who wonder what is the secret to her dedication, hard work, and her sixty years of positive contribution to the world when she said:

> *I know just how much I rely on my faith to guide me through the good times and the bad. Each day is a new beginning. I know that the only way to live my life is to try to do what is right, to take the long view, to give of my best in all that the day brings, and to put my trust in God. I draw strength from the message of hope in the Christian Gospel.*

Whether on a small or grand scale, my dad, Martin Luther King, Barack Obama, Malala Yousafzai, and Her Majesty have demonstrated strong leadership in a life dedicated to service. They have impacted the world in so many ways. I believe their faith in a higher power has influenced how they view the world and its people.

I suffer the fragilities of being human. Even though I love God deeply, in moments of weakness, I have questioned His love for me. When I experienced the pains of racism and discrimination, there were times when I felt He abandoned me. I was often gripped with anger and fear. I questioned God and religion because I was angry and fed up. Fed up with always having to be on guard against racist behaviour.

I dealt with my feelings of anger, doubt, and despair by looking deep within myself and searching for the essence of goodness. For me that is the voice of my God. I began to focus on love, compassion, kindness, and forgiveness. I discovered that my foundation was shaken with my doubts and anger, but not broken. I did not give up, because I did not want anger to rule my life. My purpose in life is driven by my faith and belief in God. On faith I set out on a very public journey, regardless of the barriers I knew I would face.

My commitment to my beliefs and faith allowed me to experience freedom from the inside out. With the inner peace there was a stillness of mind and spirit. The inner voice guided me in all my decision making. It steered me in the direction to accomplish my vision. I sought to promote unity and strength in diversity, to support equity and dignity for all people.

As a leader in the secular world who believes in God, I am mindful of the words of St. Paul in Colossians 3:12: "You are the people of God; he loved you and chose you for his own. So then, you must clothe yourselves with compassion, kindness, humility, greatness, and patience." And in Colossians 3:15: "the peace that Christ gives you in the decisions you make...it is to this peace that God has called you together in the one body."

I wanted to create a path for others to follow. I believe leaders who have a strong spiritual belief have a role to play in society. These leaders are not only confined to ordained clergy, priests, rabbis, imams, or theologians. I certainly do not fit into any of those categories. I am, however, a Christian woman of faith. I embrace and acknowledge the power of prayer. I respect religious beliefs of others. And I also respect those who do not hold any religious beliefs.

There is in my view opportunity for politicians, bureaucrats, and business and university leaders to embody the principles and characteristics of spiritual and ethical leadership in their professional life. Ethical spiritual leadership must move beyond the walls of religious institutions. We must be prepared to be leaders regardless of our creed, whether that leadership is on a large or small scale. We all have a role to play in making our communities a welcoming and economically vibrant place to live and grow. Spiritual leaders, as well as those who do not consider themselves spiritual, must have vision, goals, courage, faith, understanding of others, humility, and a strong sense of self. Love must be in their hearts along with a desire for truth and justice. The ability to listen and to communicate their message effectively is paramount. They must be knowledgeable and aware of their surroundings.

As a leader I am grounded in ethical and spiritual beliefs. I am not afraid to be visible. Dr. Martin Luther King, in a speech he delivered on March 25, 1968, said: "Somebody is saying stand, so I guess I'll have to stand."

Without my foundation in my spiritual beliefs, I am not certain if I would have been able to manage the many storms and barriers I faced along my journey. My faith in God is my shield and my armour. The road was not always easy, but I am proud to stand.

This memoir has helped me to bring to the surface feelings I have hidden for a long time. While memories of some events are painful, I had to face them if I wanted to heal. For me life is about forgiveness, love, respect, courage, kindness, empathy, honesty, compassion, giving back, and helping others.

It is my hope that my story will inspire you to realize that you can bypass barriers and reach your goals. Hard work, continuous learning, and belief in oneself will eventually yield positive results. You must never give up. You must not allow anyone to take away your dignity or break your spirit.

For those people who are angry or who perpetuate hatred, which can manifest itself in many ways, I hope you will go deep within your heart and minds and evaluate who you really are and ask the question, why am I this way? What do I need to know to be a better human being? Only the truth can set you free.

As a Black, disabled woman, I regularly review my personal strategies to get to where I believe God wants me to go. I worked tirelessly and fought hard to prevent anyone from breaking my spirit or blocking my road to success. To have my journey culminate in the heights of lieutenant-governor has taught me a great deal not only about myself but also about life and people. Regardless of the barriers placed in front of us there is always a way to survive. It may not seem that way when we are going through difficult times. There will always be times when we will throw our hands into the air and ask, why am I putting up with this? Believe me, I have been there. I relied on my God, my family, my friends, my mentors, my advisors, and my cat Angel to help me weather many of the storms I faced at different times in my life. These were my anchors. I hope you will find yours.

Rocky, I think this memoir answered your question. Thank you for being one of the warriors upon whose shoulders I stand. Rest in peace.

ACKNOWLEDGMENTS

I offer my thanks to my beloved family in the United States and Canada who have always supported me in my journey. They did not hesitate to answer the many questions I asked during the writing of this memoir. Many times my questions took us down memory lane, which either made us laugh or feel sad.

Writing my memoir was not easy. I am grateful to my close friends (you know who you are) in Buffalo, NY, New York, Halifax, and Toronto who demonstrated their patience and love for me. They made me smile and inspired me to keep writing.

To Dalhousie University, I owe a debt of gratitude. Being appointed in 2015 as a distinguished public service fellow with the Faculty of Management School of Public Administration gave me the structure and support needed to tell my story. I was fortunate to have as my research assistant one of our graduate students, Irina Wandera, from Kenya, who has since graduated and returned home. Irina was an amazing researcher. I thank her for her dedication and hard work.

A special thanks to editor Marianne Ward for her patience, her attention to detail, dedication, determination, and words of encouragement, which made the editing process something that I was proud to have experienced.

Thanks to Nimbus Publishing & Vagrant Press, especially Whitney Moran, managing editor, for publishing my memoir. I will be forever grateful.

I thank talented ladies' wear designer Fredrick S. Simpson, who designed the outfit—including the hat—you see on the cover of this book. He lives in Brooklyn, New York.

I thank my precious but mischievous cat, Noah James, for distracting me when I needed to take a break.

I thank all of my ancestors who fought for freedom and justice. I stand on their shoulders. Without their struggle for human rights, there would be no story for me to tell.

Lastly, I thank God for the many blessings that have been bestowed upon me. The publication of my memoir is another blessing.

APPENDIX

Additional Activities and Awards

Interviewed for the documentary film *Africville in Black and White*, produced by Cyrus Sundar Singh and Juanita Peters, which debuted at Hot Docs Film Festival in Toronto in May 2017 and at FIN Atlantic International Film Festival in Halifax in September 2018

Narrated *Legion Magazine*'s Military Moment video, *Canada's First Black Battalion*, on the No. 2 Construction Battalion, February 2017

Profiled in *Maclean's Magazine*, special Canada Day issue, Canada's Stories in July 2016

Chair, Atlantic School of Theology (2015–2017)

Monthly columnist for *Halifax Herald* newspaper (2004–2006)

Featured in *Canadian Who's Who*, Grey House Publishing Canada

Member of Board of Directors of Imagine Canada (2004–2005)

Invited guest for speeches by President George W. Bush and Prime Minister Paul Martin at Pier 21, Halifax (2004)

Member of Canadian National Institute for the Blind General Council (2003–2004) and Governance Committee (2004)

Invited guest for state dinner in honour of South African President Thabo Mbeki at Museum of Civilization, Gatineau, QC (2003)

Profiled in *Globe and Mail* special supplement for Congress of Social Sciences and Humanities (May 2002)

Featured in inaugural *Black Who's Who in Canada,* Dawn P. Williams (self-published, 2002)

Profiled in the cover story of the Fall 2001 edition of *Maroon and White*, the alumni magazine of Saint Mary's University

Recipient of an award from the Multicultural Education Council of Nova Scotia for exemplary contributions and commitment to improvements in the area of race relations (June 2001)

Member of Privy Council's external Advisory Group on Diversity in the Federal Public Service (2000)

Member of Nova Scotia's Voluntary Planning Board (2000)

Recognized by the Congress of Black Women of Canada, Preston, Nova Scotia, and Area Chapter for outstanding work in human rights (2000) and for "making a difference in the community" (1994)

Presented human rights award at the 4th Annual South African Women for Women Award Ceremony (2000)

Featured in commemorative book *Millennium Minds: One Hundred Black Canadians*, W.P. Holas, Pan-African Publications (2000)

Member of the Board of Governors for University College of Cape Breton (1999)

Member of Zonta International, Halifax Chapter (1991)

Honorary Degrees and Other Honours

Named one of 52 "Dalhousie Originals" for 200th anniversary of Dalhousie University, 2018

Atlantic School of Theology, Doctor of Divinity (Hon.) 2018

Acadia University, Doctor of Civil Law (Hon.) 2018

Dalhousie University, Doctor of Laws (Hon.) 2016

Nova Scotia Community College, Honorary Diploma, 2016

Awarded World Peace Tartan, Celtic Cultural Society of Nova Scotia, September 2016

Distinguished Public Service Fellow, Faculty of Management, School of Public Administration, Dalhousie University 2015

York University, Doctor of Laws (Hon.) 2014

Saint Mary's University, Doctor of Civil Law (Hon.) 2012

University of West Indies, Luminary Award 2010

Mount Saint Vincent University, Doctor of Humane Letters (Hon.) 2008

Order of Nova Scotia 2006

PERMISSIONS

"Ailey, Baldwin, Floyd, Killens, and Mayfield (When Great Trees Fall)" from *I SHALL NOT BE MOVED* by Maya Angelou, copyright © 1990 by Maya Angelou. Used by permission of Random House, an imprint and division of Penguin Random House LLC. All rights reserved.

Excerpt from *Revolutionary* by Burnley "Rocky" Jones (Roseway, 2016).

Excerpt from *Nova Scotia Human Rights Commission: 25th Anniversary: A History 1967-1992*, Bridglal Pachai, ed. (The Commission, 1992).

Excerpt from *Go to School, You're a Little Black Boy: The Honourable Lincoln M. Alexander: A Memoir*, Lincoln Alexander with Herb Shoveller, (Dundurn, 2010) 132, 135.

Excerpt from *Viola Desmond's Canada: A History of Blacks and Racial Segregation in the Promised Land*, Graham Reynolds, (Fernwood, 2016).

Excerpt from "The Dress: Mayann Francis and the Call to Serve, 2 September–27 November, 2016," courtesy Dalhousie Art Gallery.

Excerpt from *From the Pier, Dear! Images of a Multicultural Community*, copyright Whitney Pier Historical Society, 1993.

Excerpt from *The Servant Queen and the King She Serves*, copyright Bible Society, 2016.